JOHN AND BETTY STORIES

Tales of

JOHN MORE AND BETTY TAYLOR MORE

Pioneers in Delaware County, New York

by

GRACE VAN DYKE MORE

Illustrated
by
VIRGINIA MORE ROEDIGER

*To all the boys and girls who can proudly claim
John More and Betty Taylor More as
ancestors, this book of stories
is lovingly dedicated.*

Library of Congress cataloguing and publication data.

First Edition Published by John More Association, 1930,
Printers: Rogers-Kellogg-Stillson Co., New York.

John and Betty Stories: Tales of John More and Betty Taylor More, Pioneers in Delaware County, New York.
Author: Grace Van Dyke More
Illustrated by: Virginia More Roediger Johnson

Second Edition Published by John More Association, Inc., 1995, printed and bound by Thomson-Shore, Dexter, Michigan.
Historical Notes by James Bolard More © 1992.
Cover jacket illustration "Crossing the Bearkill" by Randy Asplund-Faith © 1995. Jacket text by Eric More Marshall.
All Rights Reserved. The dust jacket illustration may not be reproduced in any form without permission in writing from the artist.
For information, write John More Association, Inc., Roxbury, New York 12474.

Key Words: Pioneers, Scottish settlers, Indians, Delaware County, New York, John and Betty Taylor More, American Revolution.

Library of Congress Catalog Card Number: 9594160

International Standard Book Number (ISBN): 0-9646105-0-7

Historical Notes

Published upon the occasion of
The One Hundred Fifth Anniversary
of the organization of
The John More Association.

I nformation revealing factual errors in *the John and Betty Stories* has been discovered since their first publication in 1930. Two biographical letters written by John More and subsequent research in Scotland by the late James Bolard More, until recently the Historian of the John More Association, include a number of new facts. When considering republishing *the John and Betty Stories* by Grace Van Dyke More, the Board of Directors of the John More Association decided that the text should not be revised. Nevertheless, it was deemed relevant and important to add these historical notes to provide information on these factual errors. The corrections were written in 1992 by James Bolard More who passed away in 1993. This republished book is dedicated in loving memory of James Bolard More, who devoted so much of his love and life to the John More Association. His memory is treasured.

The following is information supplied by James Bolard More:

Pages 11 and 12: In John More's letter to his son John T. More in 1837, John More stated that he "was born in Forres Feb'y. 24th, 1745. My father and family moved to Strathspey in 1748 where I was raised and got an education."

According to Scottish records, John More Sr. owned land and a house behind the parish church in Forres, Invernesshire from 1746 to 1780. Forres is located on the Moray Firth twenty three miles east of Inverneess and eleven miles west of Elgin in the Scottish Highlands. He probably occupied this land before then and apparently maintained his ties with Forres after moving south to Strathspey.

He was a squarewright, a carpenter and builder in Forres. According to the Seafield Muniments at the Scottish Record Office in Edinburgh, John Sr. worked as a sawmiller and millwright (a builder of mills) for the Laird of Grant in Strathspey from 1744. According to John More's letter, his father did not move his family from Forres until 1748. After departing Forres, John More Sr. moved south to Coulnakyle, a farm near Nethy Bridge in the Parish of Abernethy, about twenty one miles up the river Spey from Forres, which would place him nine miles north of Rothiemurchus, where his son, John More settled. While at Coulnakyle, John More Sr. saw the births of his younger children, Isabel, James, and David.

In 1766, at Dell in Abernethy, John More Sr. built a "boring mill" to bore logs as water pipes, for shipment to London. His son John More built a similar boring mill for the Laird of Rothiemurchus shortly thereafter. Both boring mills were failures, but John More remained as a sawmiller for the Laird of Rothiemurchus until his departure for America in 1772. His father and brothers moved to the Dell of Rothiemurchus before 1772, and later to Inverdruie.

Still later, David More lived at the farm of Drumchork in Inverdruie, which is on the present day Rothiemurchus Estate two miles east of the town of Aviemore. John More lived in the Boring Mill Cottage at the burn of Aldracardoch in Rothiemurchus. Today the Rothiemurchus Estate is managed by John Peter Grant, the fourteenth Laird of Rothiemurchus.

Page 21, line 30: the word "poltroons" should read "patroons."

Pages 25-53: The Harpersfield farm (in the Catskill mountains of New York State) was not quite as isolated as indicated in the original John and Betty Stories. The farm was only two or three miles from the Harpersfield settlement. In August, 1775, John More, with the Harpers and others, signed the Articles of Association in support of the Continental Congress. In his letter to Capt. Barent Dubois in 1834 regarding his Revolutionary War service, John More stated that he served as a private in the Militia under Captain Alexander Harper from 1776 and that, because of Indian raids, they had to evacuate the settlement in April, 1778. He moved to Catskill Landing and served in the Militia under Capt. Benjamin Dubois until the end of the war. He also used a schooner and carried supplies to the American garrison at West Point for eight months in 1780 and 1781.

Pages 53-55: The story of the warning by Joseph Brant and the escape from Harpersfield was told in Jay Gould's History of Delaware County, published in 1856 (pp.68-72). It is much the same as told by Grace Van Dyke More except that there were four children instead of three. Jonas More, the fourth child, was only a few weeks old and was carried in his mother's arms, while Alexander Taylor More, aged three years, rode pillion behind his mother. It was Alexander who fell into the creek and had to be rescued by his father, John More. Jay Gould had this story from his grandfather, Alexander T. More, himself and so printed it in his publication.

Page 58: The uncle who left a legacy to the children was not Robert Taylor, but John Taylor, who died in November 1781. John Taylor was a seedsman (a seller of seeds) in the Strand in London. A copy of his Will exists, which indicates he left, among other things, 200 pounds sterling to "my sister Elizabeth Taylor, otherwise More, spouse to John More, millwright, now in America" and 500 pounds sterling to her children. In June 1788, on a petition by his five eldest children, John More was appointed their guardian by the New York State Chancery Court to collect this legacy on their behalf. Apparently, shortly thereafter John More traveled to Scotland to collect these funds.

These factual changes do not in any way detract from the atmosphere and inimitable style of Grace Van Dyke More's children's stories.

James Bolard More
Historian

November 18, 1992
Black Mountain, North Carolina

CONTENTS

FOREWORD 4

PREFACE 6

IN BONNY SCOTLAND 9

NOW WE ARE READY FOR OUR STORY 11

A STRANGE LAND 16

A LITTLE BOY IN A PIONEER HOME 25

RED NEIGHBORS 41

IN TIMES OF WAR 50

FAMILY LIFE 61

AROUND THE EVENING FIRE 74

ALONG THE SUNSET TRAIL 84

FOREWORD

. . . . *The Author has asked me to write a Foreword to these Stories. I am both honored and glad to do so.*

. . . . *If these Stories have anything like the charm for other readers, which they have had for me, the Author will enjoy our everlasting gratitude and appreciation, individually and as a clan, for her devotion and fine work in writing them.*

. . . . *When the More Family Association was organized there were many descendants living who personally knew John More and some of his children, and heard from their lips the Story of their lives. It would have been far easier then to gather the material and write such a book than at this time.*

. . . . *Grace Van Dyke More has had no help from such source. She has been obliged to gather bit by bit from one and another of those of later generations the facts for these Stories and to devote time and research to verify much that is written.*

. . . . *The style, spirit, purpose and effectiveness of these Stories in presenting pictures of the hardships, deprivations, accomplishments, sterling qualities and character of John and Betty is most admirable and convincing, and the reading of these Stories must impress us anew with the superb quality and character, the industry and courage, the honesty and earnestness, the patriotic and God-revering qualities of John and Betty and deepen our gratitude, respect and veneration for them, their lives and service.*

. . . . *On behalf of our Association, I sincerely thank Grace Van Dyke More for this, her labor of love and devotion, in giving us these cherished and charmingly told Stories of the founders of our family in America.*

. . . . *The Author was anxious to have a few illustrations in these Stories and efforts were made to enlist the talent of the family for this purpose. We were quite discouraged until Miss Virginia More Roediger, who knew of the Author's desire, sent a few illustrations, modestly disclaiming any experience or training in such work.*

. . . . *We were pleased with these illustrations, our publisher was pleased with them and the Author and the Publication Committee desire here to express their gratitude and appreciation to Virginia More Roediger for her kind, timely and artistic assistance.*

. . . . *and thank Hermon More for the picture at page 60 received as this book was to go to press.*

TAYLOR MORE.

DATED, NEW YORK, JUNE 10, 1930.

[5]

TO ALL WHO READ THESE STORIES

. . . . *This little book is the outgrowth of a story which some of you heard me tell at the More Family Reunion in 1925. I was asked to expand that story into a group of stories that would tell the boys and girls of our large family how John and Betty and their two children came to this country, how they lived, how they got their food and clothing, what they did and thought, and something about their neighbors. And so here are the stories!*

. . . . *It is difficult for us to imagine these things as they really were, for our lives and our experiences are as different as though we were living on a different planet. I have read a great deal about the world that John and Betty knew, and have tried to picture it for you in this book of tales. These stories are just as true as I can make them, and all the people in them are real people.*

. . . . *May I ask that when you read this little book you try to forget all the things that you are so familiar with—stores, schools, churches, doctors and nurses; all the comforts that we enjoy every day; steam heat, electric lights and the many, many electrical things we use; phonographs, radio, automobiles; even the street cars, busses and railroad trains—forget all these things that are so common in our world, and then try to see the world that John and Betty lived in? If you can do that, I am sure you will see the beauty, the strength, the power and the wonder of the lives of these folks whom we all can proudly claim as ancestors.*

. . . . *I wish here to express my sincere gratitude to the many cousins who have helped me with their criticisms and their suggestions during the writing of these simple tales, and especially to Prof. Edward Fitch, Carrie E. More, Anna Palen, Dr.*

Luzerne Coville, Frederick V. Coville, Milton Greenman, my brother and his wife—Mr. and Mrs. Carrol T. More, my mother, Mrs. E. J. More, who has been my most severe and most helpful critic, and our faithful President, Taylor More, who has been a constant source of inspiration and encouragement and guidance.

Yours very sincerely,

GRACE VAN DYKE MORE.

GREENSBORO, NORTH CAROLINA,
MAY 24, 1930.

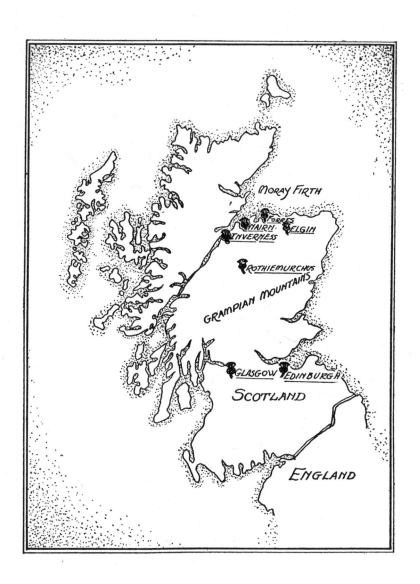

MORAY FIRTH

FORRES
NAIRN· ·ELGIN
INVERNESS

ROTHIEMURCHUS

GRAMPIAN MOUNTAINS

GLASGOW EDINBURGH

SCOTLAND

ENGLAND

IN BONNY SCOTLAND

BEFORE I begin my stories about John and Betty, let us look at this map. It is much like a map in the big geography that you study at school. How small the British Isles seem compared with the big continent of Europe, and how they seem to nestle close in the curve of the western coast of Europe as if they were quite too small to venture far out in the ocean by themselves! If you look closely, you will see that these British Isles are divided into four smaller parts, or countries, somewhat like our states. Many, many years ago each of these countries was an independent nation with its own ruler. Now, as for many years in the past, all belong to Great Britain.

. . . . Our map tells us that the lower or southern part of the larger island is England, and the upper or northern part of the island is Scotland. Then the tiny little slice over at the western side of the large island is Wales, and the smaller island that snuggles close to the western shore of the larger island is Ireland. It is Scotland in which we are especially interested. Perhaps you are wondering why I have called it "bonny" Scotland? Before we go on with our story I will tell you.

. . . . "Bonny" is a Scotch word that means beautiful, and those who have visited Scotland tell us that it is truly a beautiful country. It is a land of rugged hills and quiet glens, or valleys, of deep woods and wide fields of grain, of beautiful lakes set among the rough hills and sparkling streams of water flowing through the peaceful glens. If it is summer, on every hand there are wild flowers

—great masses of purple heather, fields of white daisies, many wild roses, and the flower we know so well—the Scotch thistle. When, in fancy, we see all this we cannot wonder that it is called bonny Scotland.

. . . . Now let us look again at our map of Scotland and we shall find, near the northeastern corner, very close to Moray Firth, a little town called Forres, and another little town farther from the water, called Rothiemurchus. If we visit Forres, we shall find it (like many other small towns in Scotland) having one broad, long street, called High Street, and all its other streets nothing more than narrow lanes branching off both sides of High Street. The houses along these narrow streets stand rather close together and look very old. They are only one story high, and the windows are small and set deep in the thick stone walls. If we walk to the western end of High Street, we shall come to Castle Hill. People who live in Forres will tell us that it is supposed that a royal castle stood on this hill many hundreds of years ago. But we shall find no castle now—nor even any ruins.

. . . . If we walk in another direction we shall find the Cherry Hills, and our Scottish friends will tell us stories of how, a thousand years ago, some women who were supposed to be witches were put to death on these hills. On the distant horizon toward the south we shall be able to see dimly the Grampian Mountains, and we shall learn that all this part of Scotland is known as the Highlands of Scotland.

NOW WE ARE READY FOR OUR STORY

A LONG, long time ago—in the year 1745 —when George Washington was a strong, fearless boy of thirteen, playing and learning and growing in Virginia, there was born, in one of those old houses in Forres, Scotland, a baby boy, who was named John More. His father, who was a skilled mechanic, was also named John. This baby John was welcomed as a playmate by two sisters and a brother. Margaret was only two years old, but Alexander was five, and Jean was a big girl of six. How these children loved the new brother, and how proud Jean was when their mother let her hold the tiny baby in her arms! . . . . When John was only three years old, the family moved to the other little town we found on the map— Rothiemurchus. This town was even smaller than Forres, for it was really no more than a group of neighboring farms. Each of these farms had a name; and the farm where John More's family lived was called Drumcork or Drumoch.

. . . . Here this little Scottish boy and his brothers and sisters grew up. They went to the village school, and John proved himself a very good student. At home he learned all the interesting things that a boy learns on a farm, and as soon as he was big enough he worked with his father until he learned all his father knew about making things, and building houses, and the boy finally became as skillful a mechanic as his father.

. . . . John's father taught the children to be proud of their name—More. He told them that it was a very old name and was a word that meant, in the Celtic language,"great" or "big." This word had often been given as a surname to men who were very large or to men who held high positions. It was first given them to describe their size or position, and then was proudly kept and used by their children, as a surname, or family name.

. . . . John and his brothers and sisters learned many other things that all children of the Scottish Highlands learned. They learned to be brave, and they learned that it is a disgrace to be a coward. They became used to hard work, and having to do without nice things they would have liked. They lived and worked and played out-of-doors so much, even in the very cold winter weather, that they grew up into strong, sturdy men and women. John learned from his father to be honest and truthful, and to keep every promise he made, but best of all, he learned to love God; and this love of God helped him through all his life.

. . . . When John was a young man—a little past twenty years old—he met a bonny lassie named Betty Taylor. Betty lived in Elgin, a short ride of twelve miles from Forres, and her home was much like the home in which John lived. She was a sweet, gentle girl, and like John, loved God, and was honest and truthful, brave and strong. Now in this story the very same thing happened that happens in all good stories—John and Betty fell in love! But John was afraid to ask Betty to marry him, because of certain longings and ambitions of his. Many other young Scotchmen were thinking and dreaming about these same things. I will tell you a little of what they were.

. . . . You remember I told you that once upon a time Scotland was an independent country with its own rulers. At that time the people were divided into clans. A clan was a group of families having the same ancestor, all living near one another, and all united under one chief who was their ruler and leader. This chief was one of the oldest and most powerful men in the clan, and the whole clan followed him in war or in peace.

. . . . About the time John More was born, this old clan life was done away with and Scotland became a part of the realm of the British King, George III. The Highlanders had always loved their independence under their clan chieftains, and they were not at all pleased with being under the rule of the English King, and under these new, hard conditions in the Scotch Highlands there was much poverty and unhappiness among all the people except the great landowners.

. . . . As a result, each year the young men of Scotland were more and more dissatisfied with their life in the Highlands and each year many of them were looking toward America as their land of hope, and were going across the great ocean to make new homes in the wilderness of this strange, wild country. John had decided that he, too, would go to America some day. Dearly he loved his home and his friends, and yet, because life was so hard in Scotland, he wanted to find a new home in some land where every man could have the same chance for a free, happy life.

. . . . No wonder he was afraid to ask Betty to marry him! Would she care to leave all her friends and go with him to that unsettled country where there would be all sorts of hardships and dangers? He feared that she would not, but finally he summoned all his courage, told her his hopes and ambitions, and asked her the great question—would she marry him?

. . . . Sweet, brave Betty! In answer to John's question she opened her Bible to the first chapter of the Book of Ruth, and read to John these two verses: "Whither thou goest I will go. Thy people shall be my people, and thy God my God." Surely Betty loved John very, very truly!

. . . . John thought he was the happiest man in the world when he heard this sweet answer. At once they began making bright plans for the future, just as all young lovers do. And so, when John was twenty-five years old, he and Betty Taylor were married, and they lived happily ever after. Sometimes that is the end of a story, but it is just the beginning of these stories, and a very nice beginning, too, I think.

. . . . John and Betty began housekeeping in Rothie-murchus and lived there for more than two years. During these years two baby boys came to make their home happier. The first boy was named John, like his father and his grandfather, but Taylor was added to his name; so in these stories whenever I am talking about this first son of John's I shall call him John Taylor. The second baby was named Robert. It was when Robert was still a tiny baby that John began to feel that the time had come when they should carry out their plan to go to

America. He talked to Betty about it, and she reminded him of her answer when he asked her to marry him, and told him that this was still her reply: "Whither thou goest, I will go. Thy people shall be my people, and thy God my God."

. . . . Knowing that each year it would be harder to break away from the old home, Betty encouraged John to go to America very soon, and they decided to start in a few weeks. Then what a busy time they had! Betty must decide what things she would take to America and what things must be left behind. Then their clothing and the few things they could take must be packed; and in the meantime all their old friends were coming to say good-bye, and to wish them God-speed on their long and dangerous journey. Betty's mother, Jean Innes Taylor, though she was seventy-two years old, came from Elgin for a visit before they left their old home. At last all was ready, and they must say their last goodbyes to their old home and to all their dear friends.

. . . . It was early autumn when John and Betty, with their two little boys and their few belongings, left their old home in Rothiemurchus and started on the long, weary journey to a strange land. There were no fine, big steamships in those days, but only small sailing vessels. So the voyage was slow and long across the rough, stormy ocean, in the little wooden vessel that rocked and pitched on the huge waves. But John and Betty kept their faces toward the west, and thought and talked of the new home they would make in the unknown, wild country toward which they were sailing.

. . . . It was early winter, six weeks later, when they reached New York, and saw the land of their hopes and desires before them.

A STRANGE LAND
"LAND AHEAD! AMERICA!"

H OW eagerly John and Betty had watched for this first sight of land! With what high hopes they gazed at the shores, as they slowly sailed up New York Bay, past the beautiful, wooded Long Island and to the landing at New York near the lower end of Manhattan Island!

. . . . With what excitement everyone on board the ship cheered when they passed the little Fort at the end of the island—Fort Amsterdam, the Dutch had called it, but the English now called it Fort George, in honor of the King. How bravely the battery of guns along the waterfront pointed their long, black muzzles out toward the great bay, commanding respect and obedience to the British rulers of this Fort! The little vessel sailed into the East River and found the end of its voyage at a dock along the waterfront on Pearl Street. Here, facing the river, beside the docks, were ship-builders' yards, and all sorts of shops and warehouses.

. . . . John and Betty were very glad to be on solid land again after the weeks of discomfort on the sea. They soon found a comfortable living place, and while Betty took care of the two little boys and put their belongings in order after the confusion of the crowded little vessel, John explored New York—all so new and strange to him. Would you like to know what he saw?

. . . . You must remember that this was in 1772, just a few years before the Revolutionary War, and that New York was a British colony that had been first settled by the Dutch many years before. John found that New York was about a mile long and a half-mile wide. About twenty thousand people lived in the town. As John walked through the narrow, crooked streets he was following the paths that used to connect the Dutch farmers' homes and fields and woods. Some of these streets were paved with small, round stones, but most of them were without pavement, and were very muddy when it rained. He noticed that all the city was kept neat, and that at night most of the streets were lighted with lamps on tall posts, instead of the old-fashioned lanterns that hung from the houses.

. . . . Although John saw some houses of wood and some of stone, he saw many others that were entirely different from any he had ever seen in Scotland. They were built of brick and had roofs of tile, and looked just like the houses in old Amsterdam. They seemed very solid and comfortable, and John was sure that honest, skillful workmen had built them. He learned that some of the brick was made nearby on Manhattan Island, but that much of the brick and tile had been brought from Holland by the Dutch who had built these houses. Many of these brick houses were two and three stories high, and

[17]

sometimes a merchant had his shop on the first floor and his home on the upper floors. The houses had no numbers on them, but each was marked by a sign of some sort, usually a sign that was appropriate to the occupation of the owner of the house.

. . . . John found that the main street north and south was Broadway, and that it extended from the Fort at the southern end of the island to the Commons, which we know as City Hall Park. North of the Commons, Broadway became a country road. He saw the most beautiful homes—those of the richest men—along Broadway, between the Fort and Trinity Church, with its slender wooden spire. He saw other fine homes on Wall Street and some on Pearl Street. There were also many shops on Pearl Street, facing the East River; but the finest shops, where the English Governor's wife and the rich Dutch ladies bought their beautiful clothes, were in Hanover Square.

. . . . John saw the best hotel, Fraunce's Tavern, which was then more than fifty years old, at the corner of Pearl and Broad Streets. It, too, was built of Dutch brick, and was one of the largest buildings in the town. Through all the years since then it has been a tavern, although the building has been altered several times.

. . . . John and Betty knew that it would not be safe to start out into the wilderness with two small children in the winter, and they decided to stay in New York until spring. This would give them a chance to learn about the different parts of the colony so that they could decide better just where they wanted to settle and build the home of their dreams. But John could not afford to be idle all winter; so he found work in a store—perhaps one of those on Pearl Street near the place where they had landed.

. . . . Little John Taylor soon found playmates among the Dutch and English children who lived near them, and baby Robert spent his days and nights growing and sleeping, and smiling and cooing, just like all good babies. Perhaps he cried a little, too, for most babies do! And Betty was a busy, happy mother, with her little family to care for, and so many new things and new ways to learn about. Each day she went to the public markets to buy food that the farmers and millers and fishermen brought there to sell; and other things she bought in the shops of the city merchants.

. . . . On pleasant Sabbath afternoons John and Betty took long walks, John carrying baby Robert, and sturdy little John Taylor toddling along beside his father. On these long walks they saw all the interesting places in the little city. At Wall and Nassau Streets they saw the City Hall, where the Council and the Court met, and where a public library was kept; and one street to the east—at Wall and William Streets—they looked at the marble statue of the English statesman, Pitt, which had been placed there just a few years before.

. . . . They liked to walk on Broadway under the beautiful trees and past the dignified homes. When they went to the northern edge of town, they found the newest church in the colony, St. Paul's Chapel, where a few years later General George Washington attended church. It was a very pretty little church and stood facing the west, on a smooth lawn that sloped down to the Hudson River, whose shore at that time was along Greenwich Street. This church still stands where it did then, but it is no longer near the water, for the land has been built out into the river.

. . . . A little farther out Broadway they came to the Commons, and were then almost in the country. Sometimes they enjoyed meeting all the townfolk here, for it was on the Commons that the people gathered for celebrations, when they sometimes roasted an ox whole for the feast, and in the evening gathered about huge bonfires and watched brilliant fireworks. If they walked beyond the Commons toward the east and north, they came to Bowery Lane, a beautiful, shaded road through the middle of the island in a country-side of prosperous farms and comfortable homes.

. . . . When they felt a bit lonely for their old home and the dear friends in Scotland, they liked to walk down to the Fort and along the sea-wall about the Battery, where they could gaze down the bay, toward the ocean and the homeland so far away. The Fort stood, fronting on Bowling Green, just where the Customs House stands now. But John and Betty could not walk in Battery Park as we can, for all of that Park is on filled land, and the water front that they knew was near the Fort.

. . . . Little John Taylor liked the great statue that stood in front of the Fort. It was a statue of the King, George III, wearing a heavy cloak, and seated on a prancing horse. There was a heavy iron railing around it, with tall supports for lanterns; so that it was light all about the statue even on the darkest nights. I am not sure whether it was the King or the horse that John Taylor liked so much, but I suspect it was the horse!

. . . . Sometimes, in the store, John met a trader who had been far back in the wilderness buying furs from the Indians, and sometimes he sold supplies to some settler who had come in from his clearing in the forest—perhaps many miles—to buy food and tools and other necessary things. John asked these men many questions about the places they had seen, about the rivers and the trails, about the soil and the trees, and about the Indians and the settlers.

. . . . John learned that the Hudson River Valley was already well settled, and that most of it was owned by Dutch and English patroons, or landowners, who held large estates that had been bought from the Indians, or given by grant of the Dutch or the English government. John knew that he would not have the chance he wanted if he stayed in this valley.

. . . . He heard many good reports about the land, the trees, and the streams in the Catskill Mountains. He was told that there were few settlers, that the Indians were friendly, and that the trees were plentiful and large. After John told Betty all he had heard, they decided to find their new home somewhere in these Catskill Mountains, and made their plans to leave New York as early in the spring as the weather would permit.

. . . . John engaged passage for themselves and their belongings on a little sloop that sailed up and down the Hudson River. This ship seemed to have no set time for starting, but sailed whenever there were enough passengers and freight to fill it. As the little boat slowly worked her way out of the dock and into the stream, there was much waving of handkerchiefs and calling of good-byes between the passengers on the sloop and their friends on shore.

. . . . Slowly they sailed northward, up the beautiful river valley, sometimes between stern cliffs and rugged mountains, sometimes between heavily wooded slopes or past homes of the Dutch and English poltroons. There they saw, through the trees or in some clearing overlooking the river, the large, comfortable houses of Dutch brick; or they caught a glimpse of a white Dutch steeple pointing

[21]

its slender finger above the treetops. They saw a few small settlements that clung close to the river's shore—Dobbs' Ferry, and Peekskill, and the big stone fort at West Point. . . . . At night the sloop was anchored near the shore, sometimes in the shadow of some dark and mysterious mountain, sometimes near one of the small settlements. By day the little boat slowly made its way northward. After several days of this slow travel, they reached the settlement at Catskill. This was the very place where, nearly two hundred years before, Hendrick Hudson had anchored his ship, the Half Moon, when he sailed up this river as far as Albany. Here, at Catskill, the friendly Indians had brought ears of Indian maize and pumpkins and tobacco, and had exchanged them for trinkets from the sailors on the Half Moon.

. . . . John and Betty stopped in Catskill long enough to buy two or three horses and some cattle and the provisions they would need. They bought large baskets, or hampers, that had been made by the Indian women; and they hung two of these on each of two horses, but the third horse was saddled for Betty to ride. In the hampers they packed their belongings—clothes, bedding, dishes, cooking utensils, tools of all sorts, food, grain and seeds for the first crop, everything that they would need for a long time. Everything had to be carried without the help of a wagon or cart, for there were no roads of any sort. Perhaps John had to put packs on the cattle as well as on the horses.

. . . . You can see that they could take only the things they positively had to have. Children often rode in the hampers I have spoken of, and probably John Taylor rode through the wilderness in this fashion, at the side of Betty's horse, while baby Robert was held close in his mother's arms. When they had packed their belongings and loaded the horses, they were ready to start on the most difficult part of their adventure.

. . . . John led the way on foot, sometimes following an Indian trail, sometimes going through a forest so thick that he had to cut away branches of trees before Betty and the children could ride under them. There were no bridges; so when they crossed a stream the horses had to ford it. Day after day they pushed on, ever westward from the river, through a wilderness of pines and hemlocks, maple and beech. Sometimes the woods were so dense that it was almost twilight in them at noonday.

. . . . When night came, they made their beds under the stars and the trees, sometimes with a rude shelter of limbs, and sometimes no shelter at all—merely their blankets over some broken boughs on the ground. Betty's heart must have been fearful as she carefully wrapped the babies in their blankets, while she listened to the dismal sighing of the wind through the trees, or the hooting of an owl in a nearby tree, or the howling of a wolf down in the valley.

. . . . John must have been constantly watchful, both by day and by night, for wild animals or for hostile Indians who would destroy his loved ones. It was not so hard to be on guard during the day, but at night it was necessary to waken often to see if all were safe. It was a hard and dangerous journey, and John and Betty had need of their brave hearts.

. . . . All along the way John was watching for a place where he wanted to settle and build that home of which he and Betty had been dreaming. At last, a mile from the West Branch of the Delaware River, and about three miles from where the town of Hobart now stands, he found a spot that suited him. There were no other settlers near, and John asked Betty if she would be too lonely so far from other families. But sweet, brave Betty assured him that she would be quite content wherever she could have her husband and her babies.

. . . . I am sure that both John and Betty loved the mountains; and perhaps this place he chose for their home looked like some dearly loved spot in bonny Scotland. There was a spring of cold water, and a clear, sparkling stream; there was level ground for a clearing large enough for house and fields; and best of all, the trees were so deeply green that John knew the soil was rich and would bear plentiful crops.

. . . . Their weary journey had brought them fifty-five miles from the nearest settlement, Catskill, and here they started their new home in the new land. They were in the town of Harpersfield, a large section of land where the Harpers were the first settlers, but the Harper's clearing was many miles from this spot that John chose for his home.

. . . . John hastily built a simple shelter of poles and branches that would protect them from the weather until he could cut trees, trim off their branches, and build a log cabin. While cooking over a wood fire in front of the open side of this shelter, helping John all she could, and caring for the little boys, Betty had little time to look at the beautiful scenery about them, or to explore the valleys and hills nearby.

. . . . When the log cabin with its great stone chimney and its roof of thick bark was finished, Betty, with a happy song in her heart, began making this rough little house into a real home for her dear ones.

A LITTLE BOY IN A PIONEER HOME

J OHN TAYLOR was not quite three years old when his father built their cabin home. In the four years they lived there, he grew to be a strong, sturdy boy, for he was out of doors most of the time in fair weather. He came to know the forest —its trees and flowers and birds, and its wild analsmi. He learned much of the Indians' habits and became a friend of the Indians who visited his father's cabin. He learned how pioneers provide the things they need without the help of factories or stores, and he began doing his small share toward providing these necessary things for the family.

The Fireplace . . . . John Taylor always loved the big fireplace of rough, gray stones. To him it seemed very large and friendly—as if it were the center of all the life of the cabin. He was so small when the cabin was built that he did not remember how his father had gathered these stones from a ledge of rocks nearby and from the ground about the spot where the house stood. Of these stones John had made the foundation for the house, and had built the great fireplace and chimney. He had no mortar; so he had to put the stones together with a sticky clay.

. . . . John Taylor thought there must always have been a fire in this fireplace, for it was always burning in the daytime, and at night was carefully covered so that there would be some fire the next morning. Over this fire Betty did all the cooking, and around this fire the family sat on long, cold, winter evenings, when outside the wind blew and the snow fell. This same fire provided all the heat they had, and many nights, all the light as well.

. . . . The little boy especially liked the evenings before the fireplace when his mother knitted warm stockings and mittens, while his father mended harness, or sharpened tools, or mended shoes for some of the family. As John and Betty worked they talked quietly, and John Taylor's eyelids grew heavier and heavier, and his head nodded more and more often. Then his mother tucked him into the little trundle-bed that, during the day, was put away under his parents' big bed, and the next thing John Taylor knew the sun was shining through the open door, and his mother was cooking breakfast over the big fire.

With John at His Work . . . . Little John Taylor was quite sure that his father was the most wonderful man in the world, for he could cut down a tree and turn it into tables and stools, or a bed, or a door—just anything he wanted to! John Taylor knew, for he had watched him do it!

. . . . He watched while his father, who seemed so big and strong, cut down a large tree and trimmed off all the branches. Then came the hardest part of all—when he slowly drove wedges of hardwood into the log and in this way carefully split it into several thick, rough boards. It seemed to John Taylor that his father was very, very slow about the next task, for it took such a long time to make these boards smooth with just his axe and knife to work with. But at last the boards were ready to use, and then John made all sorts of useful things, while the little boy watched and asked many questions.

. . . . It was fortunate that John had learned, from his father, in Scotland, how to do all these things. He needed all his skill, for besides building the cabin, he had to make nearly all the furniture they had—tables, stools and beds, and a cradle for the baby. He made the strong, heavy door of the cabin and hung it on big leather hinges, and even the floor of the cabin was as smooth and even as John could make it with the few tools he had.

. . . . He had no nails to fasten things with; so he had to bore a hole with a gimlet or small augur, and then make a wooden peg that would just fit the hole—and this peg took the place of a nail. All this meant long, patient hours of work.

. . . . Then there was often harness that must be mended, or new harness to make, or tools that must be sharpened, or new handles to be carefully cut from very hard wood, and put on the tools, or there were bowls to be carved out of wood for Betty to use when making butter or storing food. In the long, twilight evenings of summer, John worked near the open door of the cabin, while Betty sat on the low doorstep with her knitting or walked beside her spinning wheel, and the little boys played nearby till their eyes were heavy with sleep.

. . . . After John had killed a deer or a fox, or any one of the many animals that lived in the woods all about them, the little boy liked to watch his father dress the skin and prepare it for use as a rug, or a warm covering in winter, or material for moccasins and other useful things.

. . . . Then there were many long, sunny days when John Taylor followed his father about his work and tried to help him. Some days John was cutting trees and making the clearing larger. Some days he was gathering stones from a new field and building them into a low wall around the field. John Taylor especially liked these days, for there were many stones he could carry, and he felt that he was helping his father a great deal. There were other days when John was ploughing his small fields and planting seeds. All these days were delightful and wonderful to the little boy, John Taylor, and each day he was more sure that his father could do anything in the whole, wide world.

Food from the Forest . . . . It wasn't always possible for Betty to prepare the sort of meals she would have liked to prepare. She could not go just around the corner to a grocery store, or telephone to the meat-market for a steak. She had to use carefully and skillfully the few provisions they had brought with them, and the food that came from the forest and the fields about them.

. . . . When meat was needed John took his gun and went into the forest, or with his fishing rod went to the nearest stream. He rarely failed to bring back meat for several good meals—a deer, a rabbit, or a turkey, some partridges, or wild pigeons, or several fish. In the spring and fall there were many wild geese on the river, and these furnished a real feast when skillfully cooked by Betty. She also saved the feathers for pillows and featherbeds to make their beds more comfortable, and the wings of the larger birds she used to brush the ashes and dust from the fireplace.

. . . . Little John Taylor wanted very much to go with his father hunting and fishing. He thought it would be so wonderful to see his father shoot the deer or take the great wolf out of the trap. But when he asked to go his father always said: "Na, na, ma wee laddie, ye're too wee. Wait till ye are a big, braw lad, and then ye may gang wie me." But John Taylor thought it took such a long time to become a "big, braw lad!"

. . . . When fruit was needed Betty went with a basket into the woods and gathered berries: in the early summer there were the sweet, red, wild strawberries; and later in the summer black cherries, luscious blueberries, and juicy blackberries, red and black raspberries, and gooseberries; and in the fall small wild grapes hung in purple clusters, and the wild plums hid their red cheeks among the friendly green leaves. In the late fall enough butternuts, beechnuts and chestnuts could be gathered to last till the next year. During the winter they had no fruit except what Betty could dry or preserve during the summer and fall.

. . . . When Betty went berrying she usually took the little boys with her, for she could not leave them alone in the cabin, and unless John were working very near the house, there was no one with whom to leave them. John Taylor liked these berrying trips—they were almost like picnics. His mother let him eat all the berries he wanted! When the way was rough, Betty carried Robert, and she was a tired mother when she reached the little cabin home with her double burden of baby boy and basket of fruit, with John Taylor proudly toddling at her side, his hands full of flowers from the abundance of the woods.

. . . . Near the streams and in the woods Betty found marshmarigolds, which she cooked for greens, and in moist places in the woods she found wintergreen, which she used for flavoring foods and as medicine. She found other plants useful in sickness—Mayapple, wild ginger and goldthread. As there was no doctor who could be called in case of illness, these were especially precious, and during the summer Betty dried some of each of these herbs for winter use.

. . . . Among the few things that Betty had brought into the wilderness were some small hop vines and roots of tansy, spearmint and peppermint. These had been given her by her neighbors in New York, and she planted them near the cabin and tended them carefully, for she must have the hops to make yeast for her bread, and the tansy, spearmint and peppermint for medicine. John had brought grain for his first planting—oats, rye and buckwheat; and seeds for his first garden—corn, beans and pumpkin, and potatoes for a first planting, and flax for his first, small field.

. . . . To provide sugar John went into the woods in the early spring and tapped the maple trees. He cut a gash three or four inches long through the bark and into the wood. From this gash, and through a deep groove down the length of a spile of basswood two inches wide and a foot or so long, the sap ran into buckets below. The sap of many, many trees was gathered; boiled in a large, iron kettle hung over an open fire; strained through a cloth; and then boiled still more until it became a rich, thick syrup. Fifty pails of sap would make only about one pail of syrup.

. . . . This syrup Betty took into the cabin and boiled still more, stirring it all the time, until it became a soft, brown sugar that looked like the brown sugar we use when we make candy, but did not taste at all like it. This sugar that Betty made was delicious maple sugar. The washings of the sugar and syrup dishes Betty kept and strained, and then set in a warm place to make vinegar.

. . . . And so John Taylor learned that if his father and mother knew where to go for food, and how to get it, the forest would supply them with much of their food and with other things they needed. But it all brought more work to the heavily burdened John and Betty.

Providing Light . . . . One cool, autumn day, when a blue haze hung over the mountains about the More clearings, John Taylor knew that something special was to be done, for there were things about the cabin that were not usually there. He asked his mother what she was going to do, and she replied: "Today, laddie, I shall make the candles that will give us light in the long evenings next winter."

. . . . "May I help, mother?"

. . . . "Yes, laddie, you may bring in the wood and make up a big fire in the fireplace."

. . . . While John Taylor ran to the big woodpile he had helped his father make, and brought in sticks almost as large as himself, his mother was busy getting things ready in the cabin. First she filled the big iron kettle with tallow, clean and white, and placed it over the fire to melt. This tallow was the fat from sheep and cattle that John had killed for meat.

[31]

. . . . While the tallow was melting, Betty measured off the wicks for the candles—each must be just the same length—and these she twisted and doubled. Then she slipped the loop of each one over a candle-rod, so that the long, twisted wicks hung down over the rod. She had several of these rods, and she hung four or five twisted wicks from each of them, and then laid the rods across two poles that were laid between two chairs.

. . . . How John Taylor wished that he could twist those pretty, white wicks as his mother did! He and little Robert watched till the wicks were all done, but he couldn't see how she was going to get the wicks inside the candles!

. . . . The fire that John Taylor built up burned brightly, and by the time Betty had the wicks ready, the tallow was melted and ready to use. Then Betty took the kettle of melted tallow off the fire, and the dipping began. One rod at a time she dipped the twisted wicks into the tallow, held them there long enough for the tallow to soak into the wicks, and then laid the rod across the two poles again. By the time all the wicks had been dipped once, the first ones were hard enough to be dipped again.

. . . . And so it went: each rod with its slowly growing candles was dipped quickly again and again, and with each dipping the candle grew a little more plump and straight until, at last, they were the size that Betty wanted them. And then John Taylor knew how his mother had got the wicks into the candles!

How to Keep Clean . . . . It was one of the first warm days of spring, and the robins were busy with nest-building and digging for worms where John had been ploughing and getting his small clearing ready to plant the grain and vegetables.

. . . . Just before John went into the field to work, Betty said to him: "I shall start the soap today, for I think the rains are past and we shall have several days of clear weather."

. . . . John Taylor's eyes shone. He did not remember that he had ever seen his mother make soap, and he wanted to see how she did it.

. . . . "Did you ever make soap before, mother?"

. . . . "Oh, yes, laddie, every year, in the spring, I have made the soap that we used the rest of the year."

. . . . "But did I ever see you make it, mother?"

. . . . "Yes, laddie, but I expect you were too small to remember it," his mother answered, as she moved about the cabin quickly and lightly.

. . . . "Mother, why do you make the soap in the spring? Why not make some in the summer or the fall?" asked the eager little boy.

. . . . "Because all this grease and fat I have saved through the winter for the soap must be used before the weather gets warm. Now, laddie, we will go out doors and get ready to make the soap."

. . . . Betty and the two little boys went out to the side of the cabin, and John Taylor thought that his mother must have changed her mind about making soap for she did such strange things!

. . . . She took a barrel that had several small holes in the bottom, and put a layer of straw in the bottom of the barrel. What could straw in a barrel have to do with making soap? When John Taylor asked his mother about this, she answered: "Just wait a bit, laddie. This straw won't make the soap, but it will help make the lye, and the lye will help make the soap."

. . . . Then—stranger still—his mother stood the barrel on a wide, sloping board, in which John had cut little grooves which would help all the drippings from the holes in the bottom of the barrel to run down to one place at the lower edge of the board, and just under this place she put a large jar. Then she filled the barrel with wood-ashes that had been taken from the big fireplace and kept dry in a shed through the long winter and early spring. When the barrel was full of ashes pounded down hard, Betty poured water over the ashes, and the little boy watched patiently to see what would happen. He wondered where the lye was coming from and what it would look like.

. . . . John Taylor was greatly excited when, after a long time, he saw something begin dripping into the jar under the barrel—drip—drip—drip—slowly, but steadily, until the jar was nearly full. It looked like clear, dark-brown water, and the little boy couldn't see how it could ever be used to make soap that would make things clean!

. . . . Many times Betty put in more ashes, poured water over them, and emptied the black-looking water from the jar into a big iron kettle. When twilight was gathering she did the strangest thing of all. She dropped a hen's egg right into the great kettle of dirty-looking water—John Taylor held his breath while he waited to see what would happen—and the egg floated on the water!

. . . . "Now the lye is made, and is strong enough," said his mother, "and you must not touch it. Tomorrow we will make the soap."

. . . . The lye looked so dirty that John Taylor didn't want to touch it anyway. But he was disappointed that there was no soap to be made that day—just ugly-looking lye.

. . . . The next day dawned bright and sunny, and after breakfast was over, John Taylor asked, "Mother, will you make the soap today? May I help you?"

. . . . "Yes, laddie, to both your questions. You may gather wood for a big fire in the yard, where we boiled down the maple syrup."

. . . . The fire was quickly started and was soon burning steadily. The big, black kettle of lye was hanging over the fire, and Betty put into it all the scraps of meat-fat and grease and tiny candle ends that she had saved through the winter. Then she said to the little boys, who stood near watching everything she did, "Now we shall watch it cook till it becomes soap."

. . . . It was an ugly-looking mixture, and it boiled and boiled, and was skimmed again and again, until all the pieces of bone and skin and candle-wicks were out of it. When it had cooked a long time, it began to look like a thick molasses candy, and soon Betty declared that the soap was done.

. . . . She took it off the fire and poured it out into earthenware crocks to cool. It looked and felt like a thick, dark-brown jelly, but queer as it may seem, John Taylor found that when his hands were sticky and dirty, this strangely-made, strange-looking soft soap would help him wash off all the dirt and make his hands white and clean!

An Adventure . . . . Sometimes, before the summer's crop was ready to harvest, Betty's slender store of flour and meal was entirely gone, and John must go to the settlement at Catskill and get provisions for his little family till his own grain was ripe. And sometimes there were things they must have which John could not make, or find in the forest, or raise in the fields. Then he must again make the hard, tiresome trip to Catskill to buy these necessities.

. . . . When John was gone on one of these trips, Betty and the little boys were left all alone in their cabin in the wilderness. When darkness fell, Betty did not know whether they would see the light of another day, or whether some savage Indians would steal out of the woods in the night and destroy them all. But bravely she tucked the children into their beds, praying for their safety and for her own, and then tried to sleep.

. . . . Oftentimes she was wakened in the night by the howling of a wolf or the screaming of a panther in the forest; sometimes the hooting of an owl near the cabin made her think that savages were signaling from the edge of the clearing while they surrounded the cabin. Those were long, long nights for Betty, and she breathed a prayer of thanksgiving when John was safe at home again.

. . . . It was on one of these trips that John had a strange adventure. He did his errands in the settlement and started home; he was walking, for his horse was heavily burdened with the food and grain and other necessary things he had bought. He went as far as he could each day, so that he might reach home as soon as possible. Sometimes he let the horse lead the way, and sometimes he went ahead, trying to find a good trail for himself and his faithful animal.

. . . . One evening, just as dusk, he stopped to make his camp for the night, and left the horse standing in the trail while he started his campfire. He gathered dry twigs, lighted them with his flint and tinder, and then added larger twigs and branches to his fire.

. . . . He was busy with this task for a few minutes, and when he had the fire burning brightly, he looked up —just in time to see his horse disappearing around a bend in the trail!

. . . . John jumped to his feet, dropping his flint and tinder, and hurried after the horse with those precious provisions on its back. But the horse was so far ahead of him when he started that it was quite dark when he finally overtook the animal.

. . . . What should he do? If he tried to go back to find his flint and tinder and make his camp for the night, he feared that he would not be able to find his belongings in the dark, and the tiny fire he had started would be burned out. If he tried to make camp where he was, he could have no fire without his flint and tinder that were far back on the trail. He dared not camp without a fire, for he would be in too great danger from wild beasts, and would also suffer from the cold.

. . . . John decided that the only thing he could do was to let the horse go on, and to follow after the animal. He was tired from his long day's journey, and hungry, too. But there was nothing else to do. So, trusting to the horse's instinct and good sense to keep the trail, he let the animal go as he wished, while John himself held the horse's tail and followed! Hour after hour—all night long—he toiled on, tired and footsore, clinging to the horse's tail, and wondering where they would be when day came.

. . . . At last the first rosy streaks of dawn appeared in the east. John anxiously looked about in the dim light, trying to recognize his surroundings. Can you imagine his surprise and his joy when he found that he was near his own clearing—near his home and Betty and the children! The faithful horse had followed the trail all night long, and had brought John safe home—weary, but alive and happy!

Visitors . . . . Day after day and month after month passed by, through spring and summer, fall and winter —and all the days were much alike to little John Taylor. There were no neighbor children to play with, and there were no near neighbors to visit. For a year and a half the children saw no white woman save their mother. There was no church, no Sunday-school or day-school, and there were no shows!

. . . . Sometimes—and this was a great event—they had a visitor. Perhaps it was another pioneer home-seeker going still farther into the wilderness to make a clearing. Then there was much talking around the great fireplace, while the visitor told John and Betty about the things that were happening in the outside world. John Taylor didn't understand much that was said, and he just couldn't keep his eyes open long after he was tucked in his little bed; so he never heard the good-nights of the visitor and his father and mother.

. . . . Sometimes the visitor was a hunter or trapper, who was going far, far into the forest after furs which he would take back to the settlements and sell. He had stopped at their clearing perhaps for the night, perhaps for a few hours only. Then little John Taylor heard such exciting stories of the wild animals and the savage Indians that he clung close to his mother for comfort and safety.

. . . . Most of their visitors were Indians, and they were treated with such kindness by John and Betty that they became friends of John and his family. Sometimes they were Indians who were passing through to some distant Indian village; but more often they were Indians who were camped for a summer and autumn of hunting and fishing along the Delaware River, and in the forests nearby.

. . . . Whether the visitor was a white man or a red man, John Taylor was always happy to see him come, and never tired of listening to the stories told around the fireplace; and he was always sorry when the visitor left the More clearing.

A Baby Brother . . . . When this little family of four had lived in their cabin home almost two years, there came a cold, January day that John Taylor never forgot. That was the mysterious, exciting day when a new baby brother came to their cabin home, the newcomer making their family number five.

. . . . John Taylor was very happy to have this new playmate come—but he was so tiny! The little boy felt that surely this baby would never be large enough to play with, like Robert, who was now a big boy almost three years old. And he had no name! John Taylor wondered if they would always call him "Baby." But soon a name was decided upon, and a fine, big name it was— Alexander Taylor—the first name after John's brother in Scotland, and the second name just like the second part of John Taylor's own name.

. . . . The white neighbors who lived far away and the Indians who stopped at the More cabin were much interested in this precious baby because he was the first white baby born in all that part of the country—in all the district that was later to be called Delaware County.

As the Years Passed . . . . So the time passed for four years. Each year John made the clearing larger, and the cabin more comfortable. Each year there were more horses and cattle in the edge of the woods near the cabin, and larger crops in the fields near-by.

. . . . John Taylor grew to be a big boy past six, and Robert a sturdy little fellow five years old, and the two-year-old baby brother laughed and grew sweeter each day, as he lay in his little cradle near the fireplace, or followed his mother about the cabin as she did her work.

. . . . And John More and Betty were proud and thankful for their pioneer home, and their healthy, happy family.

RED NEIGHBORS

I HAVE already told you that many of the visitors at John More's cabin home were Indians. Perhaps you would like to know more about those red neighbors and how they lived.

. . . . All this great country of ours was the home of the Red Man for untold years before the white man crossed the ocean and found this strange land and called it America. Many, many tribes roamed the hills and plains, made war upon one another, grew stronger, or grew weaker and became parts of other tribes. The Indians living in the part of New York State where John and Betty made their home belonged to the great Iroquois group, which was made up of six tribes joined together in what were called the Six Nations. These tribes were the Mohawks, Oneidas, Tuscaroras, Onondagas, Cayugas and Senecas. Each tribe lived its own life until war came or some other very great, unusual emergency. Then their chiefs and wise men met about a great council fire and decided what they should do, and the Six Nations worked together as if they were one tribe. The Indians who roamed and hunted and fished nearest John More's clearing were of the Mohawk tribe.

. . . . A Mohawk family lived in a "long house," which was really a large cabin from fifty to one hundred feet long and fifteen or twenty feet wide. It was built on a framework of stout poles set in the ground, with horizontal supports to make the framework strong. Sometimes the roof was pointed and sometimes it was rounded. The whole house—sides and roof—was covered with thick bark, and a second framework was built around the outside to hold it all firm. There were no windows, and only one door, which was in one end.

. . . . This "long house" was divided into rooms which were on the long sides of the house, each room being six or eight feet square, with skins hung up for partitions. This left a passageway or hall down the center of the house. Each little room was the home of a family, and all the families in the long house were related to each other. Fires were built in the passageway or hall, and four families cooked and kept warm over each fire.

. . . . There were no chimneys—merely smoke-holes in the roof above the fires. Each smoke-hole had a cover of bark which could be pushed up with a long pole, or let down over the hole to keep the rain and snow from coming down on the fire. These smoke-holes allowed part of the smoke to get out of the long house; but with so many people living close together, so many fires, so much cooking, and no windows or chimneys, I'm sure a "long house" must have been a gloomy, smoky home for Indian boys and girls. Perhaps they did not mind this as we should, because they were out of doors so much more than we are.

. . . . We sometimes think that Indian men were lazy and made their squaws do all the work, but this is not entirely true. To be sure, the men did spend their time fighting and hunting and fishing, but this was necessary work, for they must often fight to protect their tribe, and they must hunt and fish to provide their family with meat to eat, and with skins for clothes and blankets. The men who were too old to fight or to hunt stayed in the camp and made the bows and arrows, tomahawks, and nets and traps for the hunters and warriors to use.

. . . . This left much work to be done by the women. They must take care of the lodges—indeed, they must often build them; they must prepare the food and clothing; and of clay that could be baked hard they must make all the bowls and jars they used for storing food and for cooking. Before they could prepare the food, they must raise much of it. So they must plant a garden in the spring and care for it through the summer till the food was ready to gather and store away for the winter. In their gardens they raised maize—which we call corn—and beans, squashes, potatoes, gourds and pumpkins. In the forest they gathered wild fruit, nuts and herbs.

. . . . They planted the maize in "hills," and as the plants grew they heaped the earth up around them. Sometimes they planted squashes or beans in the hills with the maize. These Indian squaws gave us a delicious food, for they taught our ancestors to make succotash, which is maize and beans cooked together. Perhaps Betty learned from her Indian neighbors to make succotash, and perhaps she learned how to grind maize into meal as the Indians did. Perhaps, too, her red neighbors taught her to make maple sugar, for the Indians, for many, many years, had camped in the woods in the early spring to make maple sugar.

. . . . During the summer and fall the squaws dried pumpkin, squash, beans, and even fish and meat, and parched maize—all for winter use. They stored this food away in bags made of deerskin or in bark baskets. Sometimes they pounded a piece of meat—usually venison, which is the flesh of deer—until it was in shreds, and then, into this raw meat, they pounded parched corn and squash seeds and sometimes dried cherries or berries. The whole mixture was carefully dried and stored away. This was called "pemmican," and was a very popular food. It was especially useful when an Indian went on a long journey as a messenger to another tribe, or when the men went on a long hunting or fighting expedition, because it was easy to carry, and a little of this dried food was equal to a large amount of other foods.

. . . . The Indian women had no dishes like ours— only jars and bowls of baked clay, baskets woven of reeds or thin splints of wood, and cups or dippers that were the thick shells of gourds raised in their gardens, hollowed out and dried.

. . . . One of the hardest tasks of the squaw was making clothing for her family. She made most of it from deer-skins, using other skins for blankets, to hang between the rooms in the long house, or to pile up for a bed. She first had to dress every skin that her husband brought to their lodge, and this is the way she did it. She laid the fresh hide on the ground, stretched it as tightly as possible, and pegged it down around the edges. As it dried it became still tighter, and while it was drying she scraped it to remove all the fat, and to make the skin thinner. She used for this work a scraper made of bone, or of stone which had been chipped and ground to just the right shape.

. . . . Then she rubbed much fat into the skin to soften it, spread more fat over the stretched skin, took out the pegs, rolled up the skin, and left it for several days. When she opened the roll, she washed the skin, and then rubbed and worked and twisted it until it was soft. Now, at last, the skin was dressed and ready to make up into dresses or coats, leggins or moccasins, or whatever might be needed. How much patience these Indian women had, and how much hard work they did to keep their family clothed and warm and fed!

. . . . Much of the clothing, especially the leggins and moccasins and the women's dresses, were decorated with porcupine quills and beads, often in very pretty designs. The beads these Indians used were made of the inner part of clam-shells: some were white and some were purple, and all were little round cylinders about one-and-a-half times as long as they were thick, and with the ends cut square. At first they had been used for ornaments only, but the Indians were very fond of the pretty beads, and whatever people are fond of they think is worth a great deal. So the Indians began to use their beads, or "wampum," as they called them, in the same way we use money—to pay for things they needed or wanted. Sometimes the wampum was worn in long strings, and sometimes it was made into belts; and, of course, the Indian who had the most wampum was the richest Indian of the tribe.

. . . . The Indian boys and girls did not have a chance to go to school and learn to read and write, but they were taught by their fathers and mothers and the wise old men of their tribe what they needed to know. The girls learned to do all the things their mothers did, while the boys learned to shoot with the bow and arrow, to swim, to jump, to throw a tomahawk, to make traps and nets, to make a spark of fire by rubbing two sticks together, and to follow the faintest trail through the forest by watching for broken twigs or the lightest marks of footsteps on the fallen leaves, and with no compass save the North Star, to find the way back to camp when far away in the wilderness.

. . . . Both the boys and the girls were taught to show no pain, and to bear any hurt silently and without showing any suffering in their faces. They learned how the birds build their nests, and how the beavers build their dams and their houses, and how to follow the tracks of the fox and the bear, the wolf and the panther.

. . . . Many times they heard the story-tellers of their tribe tell the ancient legends of their people—stories that sound strange to us, yet often very beautiful, too. The story-tellers told them that fire was a giant who was fed on tiny spirits who lived only in the wind, and that to blow one's breath upon the embers to make them burn more brightly was very "bad medicine." They learned to call the sun the smiling face of the Great Spirit, and thought that at sunset he entered the door of a great wigwam, and in the morning came out at the other door of the wigwam. They were taught that the moon was a sister of the sun, and that sometime she would be able to give as much light as her brother, the sun.

. . . . They were told, in a story, how the streams of water and the springs they come from were first made to provide water for the Great Spirit when he came to make a journey over the earth. Before he left the Happy Hunting Grounds on this journey he sent a great white bird to carry water from the original spring near the Great Spirit's wigwam, and plant it in the earth at convenient places, ready for the Great Spirit's coming. They thought that places where there are no springs were not visited by the Great Spirit.

. . . . As they sat around the evening camp-fire they heard from the old story-teller many wonderful tales about the birds and animals, the stars, and rain, clouds and snow, the flowers and the trees.

. . . . This is one of the beautiful legends to which they listened: "An old and honored chief went alone to the top of a high mountain to meet the Great Spirit. The chief told the Great Spirit that his people were tired of the food they must eat—roots and herbs and wild fruit —and he asked the Great Spirit to send them some of the food they used in the Happy Hunting Grounds. The Great Spirit told the chief to take his wife and all his children and in the moon of rains go forth to one of the plains and there stay without moving for the space of three suns. Then the Great Spirit would come and give the Indians food.

. . . . "The chief went back to his people and told them what the Great Spirit had said, and when the moon of rains came he did as the Great Spirit had directed. At the close of the three suns the old chief and all his family had fallen asleep, but his people did not disturb them, for they thought this was a sign of special favor from the Great Spirit.

. . . . "In a few weeks the old chief and his wife and children had changed into beautiful green plants. The council of the tribe gathered, they sent wise men to visit the field, and they found growing there maize—a food quite good enough to be eaten by the Great Spirit in the Happy Hunting Grounds. And thus the Great Spirit gave this good food—maize—to his children on the earth."

. . . . I will tell you one more legend of the Iroquois Indians—one that I am sure the boys and girls must have liked very much.

. . . . "Long ago when the animals had tribes and chiefs like the Indians, the porcupine was made chief of them all because nothing could hurt him. He called a great council of the animals, and when all were seated in a circle about the council-fire, he asked them, 'Shall we have night all the time, or daylight?'

. . . . "The animals could not agree. There was much talking, for some wanted it to be always night, while others wanted to have day always. The bear with his big gruff voice kept chanting: 'Always night. Always night.' The little chipmunk with his shrill loud voice kept singing, 'Light will come. Light will come.'

. . . . "Each animal told what he wanted, but as they all talked at once, only those with the loudest voices could be heard. They could not decide what was best, and before anyone realized the night was past, the sun began to rise, and the chipmunk was still saying, as loudly as ever, 'Light will come. Light will come.'

. . . . "This made the bear and many other animals very angry. The chipmunk saw this, and he saw, too, that what he said was coming true—the light was coming—so he decided he might as well go home, and he began to run to his nest. The bear said that this was because the chipmunk was afraid, and the bear began to run after the chipmunk.

. . . . "The great bear was very clumsy, and the little chipmunk was quick. However, the bear nearly caught the chipmunk just as the little fellow ran into a hole in a hollow tree. The bear struck him, and the black stripes down the chipmunk's back show where the bear hit him with his great paw.

. . . . "The chipmunk and his friends had won, and night and day have come ever since that great council."

. . . . Perhaps some of John and Betty's red neighbors who could speak some English told these very stories and others to little John Taylor and Robert and baby Alexander when the Indians visited John's clearing. Are you wondering how it happened that some of the Indians could speak English?

. . . . For many years before John and Betty came to America the Indians had been selling furs to Dutch and English traders, getting beads and cloth and guns and knives in return. Some of the Indians had visited the white men's settlements, and most of them had seen and met white men. So they had learned many English words, as the white men had also learned many Indian words. A few Indians learned to speak English very well.

. . . . One of these was Joseph Brant, who has been called "the greatest Indian of whom we have knowledge." When young, he was sent by some English settlers who saw that he was a bright boy, to a school in Connecticut, where he was given a good English education. He probably taught many Indian boys to speak English. This Joseph Brant was one of the red neighbors who often visited John More's cabin, and the two men—the red man and the white man—became good friends. In another story I shall tell you how Joseph Brant proved his friendship for John More.

[49]

IN TIMES OF WAR

WHILE John and Betty were living in their pioneer home, far from other settlers, in the cities and more thickly-settled parts of the colonies and in far-away England many things were happening that were destined to change the lives of these Scotch pioneers in their simple little home.

. . . . The same overbearing, unfair rule of King George III that had made life in Scotland hard for men like John More, was making trouble for all the people in the American colonies. The King persuaded Parliament, the law-making body of England, to pass laws which the colonists refused to obey, because through these laws, in some cases the colonists were being tried by the King's agents without a jury, the colonists were not allowed to buy or sell goods in any country save England, and the taxes they were asked to pay on tea, sugar, molasses and paper were unjust; and the King and Parliament would allow the colonists no vote on the matter, and would not even listen to their protests.

. . . . This trouble had started before John and Betty left Scotland, but no one expected it to lead to war between England and her American colonies. From the traders and settlers who stopped at John's clearing while going to or from the settlements near the Hudson, John heard of these things, though usually months after they had happened. In this way he heard of the Boston Tea Party, the First Continental Congress, the midnight ride of Paul Revere, the battles of Lexington and Concord and Bunker Hill, the signing of the Declaration of Independence, and other things you have read about in your history.

. . . . It did not seem possible that these happenings in Boston and Philadelphia and other distant places could affect John More and his family living so far away in the mountain wilderness. But the sounds of war echo to the farthest corners of the land, and not one man or woman, boy or girl can escape its dangers and sorrows.

. . . . While John More had always treated the Indians kindly, and had been generous with his food, yet he knew that they were very dangerous neighbors and that their anger and vengeance might turn against him at any time. Some of the Indian tribes helped the colonists in their disagreement with England, some did not take sides at all, but many helped the Tories—the colonists who sided with the British.

Preparing for War . . . . Most of the settlers about Harpersfield were loyal to the colonies; and they knew that they must stand together and be willing to fight together, if necessary. In August, 1775, about four months after the battle of Lexington and Concord, these men of Harpersfield met and declared their approval of what the Continental Congress had done, and promised to support whatever that Congress did in the future. They declared that any settler who would not join them should be banished from the colony and his property taken by the colony.

. . . . Then they chose a vigilance committee which was to watch the Tories and the hostile Indians, and to keep in touch with other groups of patriots in the colony of New York. All this was put in writing, and each man signed it. John More was one of the signers, in fact, some think that it was John who did the actual writing. This act was one of the bravest things those men could do, for it took the same sort of courage to sign this paper that was shown by Jefferson and Franklin and the other men who signed the Declaration of Independence.

. . . . The days that followed were filled with uncertainty and anxiety. John and Betty did not know what day the Tories would encourage the Indians about them to go on the war-path to kill and burn wherever they might pass. John must bravely go about his work and try never to leave Betty and the children unprotected, especially at night, and Betty must make use of all her faith and all her courage each day.

. . . . Sometimes, at night, when she was putting one of the little boys to bed, she would say to him: "Noo, laddie, say ye're prayers and gae to sleep. God only knows whether ye'll see the light of another morn', but if ye do, sonnie, and live to be a grown mon, be good, be honest and upright in your deal, and true to the God who made you."

An Indian Raid . . . . The spring days passed, John's crops were planted and growing, June came, and suddenly—without warning—the red men went on the war-path! A band of Indians and Tories, led by Joseph Brant, the Mohawk, raided the country, killing the white settlers and driving off the cattle and horses. They were coming toward John More's clearing, and were leaving death and ruin in their trail. But John and Betty, far from other settlers, knew nothing of the raid.

. . . . Of all the Indians to whom John and Betty had been kind, there was one who did not fail them in their time of danger. Joseph Brant remembered his kind, white friend, and because he did not want to have John or his family killed by the savages, in the darkness of night he slipped away from the Indian camp, crept stealthily through the forest to John More's clearing, and when near the cabin, gave a peculiar call.

. . . . John heard this call and knew that Joseph Brant was calling him. He stepped out doors into the darkness and found his Indian friend waiting for him. Brant spoke in a low voice: "The Indians are raiding—they are killing and burning. I shall not be able to hold my men back when they come here. Take your squaw and your papooses and go into the forest, and go quickly. The Indians must not know that I have warned you."

. . . . Without waiting for an answer, the Indian slipped back into the shadows of the forest—and was gone. John hurried into the cabin and repeated to Betty the warning he had heard. They were broken-hearted at the thought of leaving their little cabin-home and clearing. But there was no time for regrets or for tears—only time for hurried preparations for leaving.

. . . . John went into the clearing and turned all the cattle loose into the woods. He saddled two horses, and hung large, woven hampers on the sides of the third horse. Betty packed these hampers with food and clothing, some small valuables, and necessary dishes and tools. Some other things they hid in a ledge of rocks near the cabin. Then they were ready to go.

. . . . John went ahead, leading one horse; on the second horse rode the two little boys, John Taylor, six years old, and Robert, five; on the third horse rode Betty holding in her arms the precious two-and-a-half-year-old baby Alexander, or Sandy, as they called him.

. . . . They went through the forest as fast as they could in the thick darkness, and by daylight they were well on their way. All that weary day they traveled, John sometimes having to chop overhanging branches of the trees to let the heavily loaded horses walk under. That night, while the little boys slept soundly, wrapped in their warm blankets, John and Betty dared sleep but little for fear the savage Indians might overtake them, or wild beasts attack them and kill them all. They could have no campfire to keep the wild animals away, for fear the Indians might see it and find them, so they suffered with the cold, also.

. . . . Starting on their way at dawn, their trail led them to the Bearkill, where they found a ford, but the banks were very steep and rather high. Everything went well with the crossing of the first horse, on which John rode, and with the second horse carrying the hampers and the two little boys. The third horse, carrying Betty and the baby, got safely down into the stream and across it, but as he leaped out on the bank, the baby Sandy slipped out of his mother's arms and fell into the water, which was all muddy from the horses' crossing.

. . . . Betty screamed, John hurried back to the river bank, and Betty cried: "Oh, John—Sandy—Sandy—Sandy has fallen into the river!"

.... John quickly rescued the baby, and as he wiped the mud out of poor little Sandy's eyes and ears and mouth, he said over and over: "Sandy, is thee dead? Is thee dead?"

.... By the time John had washed off the mud and put dry clothes on the baby, Sandy was found to be still a very lively, lusty Scotch baby—quite unhurt by his mud bath!

.... They continued on their way, and at the end of four days of hard travel they reached the Dutch settlement of Embach, four miles from Catskill, the settlement from which they had started their journey into the wilderness four years earlier. They were welcomed by the kindly Dutch settlers, and were made comfortable by the Van Ordens, who had become their friends when they were buying their supplies in Catskill four years before. How thankful Betty was to be under a roof once more, and to know that her dear ones were safe from the cruel Indians!

.... As soon as John had Betty and the children settled, he went back to their clearing to learn the fate of the cabin and of their stock. When he was well along on his way he met a band of Tories and Indians driving a number of cattle, among which he recognized some of his own animals, but he dared not claim them. These men bore John no ill-will and did not offer to harm him, but at the point of a bayonet, the Tories made him promise that he would tell no one that he had seen them. John said afterward that he promised with his lips very quickly, but he said to himself in his heart that he would tell the first man he saw!

.... He went on to his clearing, meeting no one else on the way, and found the cabin in ashes, and the stock all gone. The animals that had not been driven away by the Indians had been killed and partly devoured by the wolves. . . . . John felt very sad as he looked about at the ruins—four years of such hard labor in the forest, all swept away in an hour's time! All gone! No, not all—for he still had his faithful, loyal Betty, and together they still had youth, and hope, and love!

. . . . John went back to Embach and bought some land just where a part of the town of Catskill now stands. His neighbors helped him build a cabin, and he began to clear the ground for crops. It was like starting all over again at making a home in America.

War Service . . . . It was August of 1779 when news arrived at Catskill that the British had taken Fort Montgomery, five miles below West Point, and were advancing up the Hudson. There was great excitement in all the countryside along the Hudson, as men gathered to prepare to protect their homes. John More helped organize a company of Minute Men, and they began drilling and getting ready to fight.

. . . . The Minute Men were a sort of home militia who were ready to go into service at any minute they were needed, and were an important part of the colonial forces. Most of their work around Catskill was guard duty, and John did his full share of this. All the Minute Men along the Hudson River were especially watchful, for they knew that the English were anxious to capture the forts along this river, since by this means they could split the colonies into two parts. The British thought that, if they could split the colonies and keep the colonists in one part from helping those in the other part, and from even knowing what was happening in the other part, England would win the war. This meant that guarding the Hudson River was very important work.

.... The war went on and on—sometimes the colonists were filled with hope of victory, and at other times were discouraged over defeats. The months passed, filled with work and privation for John and Betty, and in addition, much anxiety over the outcome of the war.

.... When they had been in Catskill less than a year, a baby boy came into their home and was named Jonas; and two years later, a baby girl was born, a sister for the four boys to love and care for. She was named Jean, for Betty's mother and for John's older sister, and her brothers thought that she was quite the nicest and sweetest baby girl in the world!

.... As the family grew larger, Betty's work and cares grew heavier, and the hours of each day seemed far too short to do all the things that must be done. She never sat down by the fireplace in the evening without some knitting or mending in her hands; and all day long she was busy with cooking and cleaning, and caring for the younger children. Sweet and patient always, she did her work each day, and found means to teach her children to be good and brave and true.

Peace Again .... When baby Jean was a year and a half old, the Battle of Yorktown ended the long, hard war, and the colonies were free from England's rule. They again gave their attention to their farms and to their commerce. John worked very hard on his small clearing, and the older boys helped all they could. But the soil was poor and the results were not very encouraging.

. . . . Again the family was made larger when less than a year after the war closed another baby boy, James, came to bless John and Betty's home.

. . . . While living near Catskill, John and Betty had received letters from Scotland and had sent letters to the friends and relatives there. They had written of their escape from the Indians, of the birth of the precious babies, and of the progress of the war. It was about the time the war closed that sad news came to Betty from Scotland: her unmarried brother Robert was dead. Betty and Robert had been very fond of each other, and Robert proved this by leaving part of his money to Betty's children. He left one hundred pounds, or about five hundred dollars in our money, to each of the five eldest children, John Taylor, Robert, Alexander, Jonas, and Jean. He made his will before James was born.

. . . . Soon after the news of Robert's death came, John More went down to New York in a little sloop, and from there sailed to Scotland to get this money for the children. He was away from home on this trip a long time, for it took about six weeks to cross the ocean to Scotland and another six weeks to come back, and there were many relatives and friends to visit while he was there. Best of all, John's mother was still living—about eighty years old—and was very happy to see her son again. When he had first gone to America his mother did not expect ever to see him again; so this visit was a great joy to her.

Back to the Mountains . . . . When John returned to America with the children's money, he put it on interest in New York City, where it remained till the children were grown. Since the war was over and the Indians were again peaceful, John and Betty were not content to stay in Catskill. They longed for their mountain clearing, and wanted to go back as soon as they could. In the meantime, on a cold January day in 1786 the seventh baby came to their home—another boy—and was named David. The next summer the family started back to the old clearing.

. . . . They had been in Catskill for nine years; there had been three children when they went to Catskill; now there were seven, six boys and one precious sister. John Taylor and Robert were almost grown—fifteen and fourteen years old—and each was ready and able to do a man's work to help his father. Betty disliked leaving her friends in Catskill and going back into the wilderness where she would have no neighbors within many miles, and she did not like to leave the settlement where they could get their mail and supplies without a member of the family having to travel for days through the forest after them. But she was always willing to do whatever was best for John and their children, no matter how hard it might be.

. . . . This trip through the wilderness was not so hard as the first one John and Betty had made over the same trail thirteen years before. The trails were better, but there was still great danger from the Indians and from wild animals. But now John Taylor and Robert could help guard their mother and the younger children; Alexander and Jonas could gather wood for their camp-fire and carry water from the nearest spring or stream; and six-year-old Jean could watch the two younger children, James and baby David, while their mother prepared their food and did other necessary work.

. . . . While on the trail toward their old clearing in Harpersfield they met a man named Clark, who owned a claim where Grand Gorge now stands; and after much discussion, John More and Mr. Clark decided to trade claims. The bargain was completed, and John and Betty and the seven children, with their horses and stock and household belongings, went on to their new claim to begin again the hard struggle to make a home and a living in the wilderness.

HERMON MORE

FAMILY LIFE

UNBROKEN forest, swift-running streams, and rolling, green hills on every side, into this wilderness again came our brave, Scotch ancestor, John More, with his wife, Betty, and seven children, a number of horses, cows, sheep, chickens and geese, the most necessary household goods, and grain and seeds and cuttings of plants and fruit trees to set out about their new home.

. . . . John and Betty had been in America fourteen years and now for the third time must build a cabin, open a clearing, and plant their crops in newly-broken soil. But they were not afraid of hard work, and were determined to have a home in this country, where the poorest man as well as the richest man has a chance.

. . . . They found the Clark claim, which was now theirs, and set to work. Again a rough bark hut was built to shelter them from storms while they were cutting logs, gathering stones, and building a comfortable cabin. But this time the work went faster, for John Taylor and Robert were working with their father. As soon as they could make a clearing large enough for crops they planted grain and vegetables and fruit trees.

. . . . The life of John and Betty and their family was here much the same as it had been on their first clearing in Harpersfield, except for one thing—this new home stood where several trails met, and was just far enough from the settlements to be a convenient place for travelers to stop for the night.

. . . . So Betty's log-cabin home became a stopping place for passing trappers, traders, and settlers. The cabin had to be made larger; and after a number of years, John built a small frame hotel, or tavern. Travelers who passed along these trails liked to stop at John More's tavern, for it was always clean and neat, John was a friendly host, and the tavern was noted for the fine meals that Betty cooked and served. In those pioneer days when rough manners and coarse language and heavy drinking were common, John did not permit these things about his tavern, and Betty's sweet, gentle ways and her good cooking often made a lonely traveler long for a home of his own.

. . . . Two years after settling on this clearing a baby boy came to John's and Betty's home—the first white boy born in the town of Roxbury—and the last one to come to John and Betty. This boy was named Edward Livingston, and his birth made John's children number eight, seven boys and one girl.

Tasks for Every Boy . . . . There were so many
things to be done about this pioneer home and tavern that the children had a chance to learn about and to do all sorts of interesting things. The first tasks of the youngest children were carrying in wood for the big,

open fireplace, picking up potatoes in the field where the men were digging them, and turning the grindstone while John or the older boys sharpened axes and scythes. The boys a little older could turn the cows out to pasture in the morning, and drive them in at night. In the early summer they helped their mother catch the geese, and helped hold them while Betty plucked off the softest feathers. When this task was finished the geese looked ragged and pitiful, but they were rid of feathers that would make them too hot during the summer, and Betty had more feathers for pillows and feather beds.

. . . . One day, while Sandy was still a small boy, his father sent him into the woods to find a horse that had strayed away from the clearing. When he was well into the woods, suddenly he saw before him a large mother bear with her two cubs. The bear was so afraid that this strange, two-legged animal might harm her cubs that she came toward the little boy growling fiercely and with mouth open wide. Sandy was terribly frightened, for he was all alone and had no weapon—only a horse's bridle in his hand. But the plucky little Scotch boy stood his ground, drove the bear off with the bridle, went on, found the horse he was looking for, and led it home.

. . . . The older boys helped their father with the spring plowing and sowing, and then later with the cutting of the grain and hay; the younger boys spread the hay to dry and later raked it up and put it into stacks. During the winter, in the barn, they helped to thresh out the oats and rye with hickory flails. When John added a new field to his clearing, the older boys helped cut the trees, while the younger boys gathered up the stones to be built in a stone wall around the field.

. . . . One of the great adventures of each year was "sugarin'," when, in the early spring, the older boys went into the woods to the sugar camp with their father, and helped him tap the maple trees, gather sap, and make the maple syrup. Through the summer there were many trips after berries of different kinds, and in the fall the great fun of nutting—gathering butternuts, beechnuts and chestnuts. The boys were as busy putting away nuts for the winter as their friends, the chipmunks, who scampered through the woods getting and hiding nuts for their winter store!

. . . . How good these nuts tasted on cold, winter nights when the family sat about the great fireplace! Often the circle was made larger by some traveler who was stopping over night. While the boys and girls roasted chestnuts, Betty sat at one side of the great hearthstone knitting mittens to keep the many pairs of hands warm in the bleak, cold, winter weather, and long, woolen stockings, or mending jackets, or perhaps turning a little flax-wheel. John sat on the other side of the hearthstone, telling stories of his boyhood in Scotland, or listening to their traveler-guest tell what was going on in the big world of cities, and of travels in far-away lands he had visited. For John's children these evening talks and stories took the place of the magazines we read, as well as of many lessons in history and geography.

Learning Without a School . . . . The children of John More's family had many happy times that boys and girls of today know nothing about. But they missed one thing we have—our schools. All they learned must be from their father and mother, but the hours and the days were too full of work to be able to set aside regular hours for teaching the children. John and Betty had gathered a few good books, including the Bible, which was the most important book of the home and in these books all the children learned to read. But if they did not get so much "book learning" as boys and girls have nowadays, they learned many things that most of us have no chance to learn.

. . . . They learned the ways of foxes and woodchucks, coons and squirrels, by hunting them; they learned how to make traps and the best places to set them to catch different kinds of animals; they knew how to find the honey of the wild bees; they learned the places where the fish would bite the best; and they knew where to find the shadiest, deepest swimming-holes.

. . . . They learned the songs and calls and the habits of many birds—the song-birds as well as the crow, the hawk, the owl and the partridge. They made friends with the robins and swallows that nested about the house and barns; they knew where the woodpecker, the wren and the oriole had their nests, full of hungry little ones; they watched the bumble-bees and the yellow jackets; and they even learned the ways of the frogs and lizards and snakes.

. . . . In winter, when there was snow everywhere and it was very cold for weeks and months at a time, they learned to tell what animals were about by their tracks in the snow, for they knew the clear-cut track of the fox, the sharp, wiry track of the squirrel, the soft-edged track of the rabbit's padded feet, and the pretty footprints of the deer mice that looked like fancy stitching on the snow.

. . . . They learned to watch the clouds and the weather, and to love the turning of the leaves in the fall, and the first faint green of the early spring. They knew where to find the sweetest strawberries, the juiciest blackberries, the largest wild cherries, the finest nuts, and the most tender wintergreen berries.

. . . . So many, many things these boys and their sister learned that we cannot learn from books, and some of the finest things that can be learned no where else so well as at home, from father and mother—such as habits of work, helpfulness to each other, love and obedience to parents, and love of God. Their father's word was to them the law, and to their father and mother they lovingly looked for final authority in all things.

Jean—a "Little Woman" . . . . While the boys learned more about things out-of-doors than Jean did, she was having a wonderful time helping her mother with all the interesting tasks about the house. All the children helped when Betty made candles, but Jean helped the most with the soap-making and spinning. She learned to cook and to bake all the good things her mother made; but the hardest thing was learning to bake in the brick oven.

. . . . It was just like the ovens that the Dutch housewives in Catskill used, and was often called a Dutch oven. It was built into the big, stone chimney beside the fireplace in the kitchen. When Betty was going to bake, she built a fire of dry wood in the oven several hours before the time she wanted it to be hot. This fire she kept burning, and when the oven was hot enough, she raked out the coals and charred wood, and put in the bread and pies and puddings. To keep from getting burned when putting things into the oven and taking them out, Betty used a flat shovel with a very long handle.

. . . . Jean learned how the cloth for most of their clothes was made, using the flax grown in their own fields, and the wool cut from their own sheep. In the early summer she watched her father and brothers shear the sheep and clean the wool, and then she helped her mother dye it, and card it, and spin it into yarn. Then it was ready for Betty and Jean to knit into warm stockings and mittens, or to be woven into cloth.

. . . . To the little girl it seemed very wonderful that some of their clothing and all their household linen came from a plant—flax—just an ordinary looking plant with pretty blue flowers, but with very strong fibres in its stems. Each year Jean saw her father cut the flax with a sickle; and then he had a slow, hard task breaking up the fibres, combing out the tow and waste, and making the good fibres clean and straight. From her mother Jean learned to spin this flax into linen thread, using a small flax-wheel. This thread, like the woolen yarn, was taken to a weaver in Catskill to be woven into cloth.

. . . . Jean knew so many things that the girls of today know nothing of. I wonder, if she were here, would she think us stupid? And her brothers! How much they could teach the boys of today, and how the boys would like to learn from them!

Time Brings Changes . . . . The years passed. John and Betty's family was growing up. Each year their clearing was larger, more stumps were taken out or burned, more stones were gathered and built into walls around newly-cleared fields, more crops were planted, and there were more cattle and horses and sheep in the pastures and barns. Gradually, through the years, the trails became well-broken, and some roads were made, sometimes following the old trails over the mountains, sometimes lower in the valley.

. . . . John More's tavern at the meeting of the trails was such a convenient stopping place that a little settlement grew up about it, and was called Moresville. Then John had more and more things to do beside running his farm and tavern. When a postoffice was needed, John was appointed postmaster, an office which he held for many years. He was also a magistrate, and in his beautiful, clear hand, wrote all the legal papers for the settlers for many miles around.

. . . . All the troubles and disputes that arose between his neighbors came to John, as magistrate, to settle. He was kind and fair in these cases, and always tried to get the men to agree and settle the matter without a trial. The neighbors who came to John for help of this sort, as well as those who came just to ask for advice, always went away satisfied, sure that his judgment was fair and honest.

. . . . Because he was a magistrate, John could perform the marriage ceremony, and during the years before there was a preacher in Delaware County, he had the joy of making happy the young people who wanted to be married. Can you imagine how excited the children were when a young couple came to the tavern and asked their father to marry them, and how the children watched with big, round eyes; or if perhaps their father did not allow them to go in and watch the wedding, how they waited near the door till the happy couple came out and rode away on horseback?

. . . . John and Betty were sorry that there was no church or minister near, and decided to do what they could to overcome this lack. John invited all the neighbors to come to the tavern on the Sabbath for worship, and when they were gathered, John led the devotions, and then read a sermon from a book of sermons he owned and loved, or sometimes he asked someone else to read the sermon. Frequently groups of people worshiped in this way during the early pioneer days.

Eight Love Stories . . . . As John's boys became men the same thing happened to them that had happened to their father so many years before in Scotland. Each one of them met a sweet, lovely girl from among the sturdy, pioneer families about Moresville, fell in love with her, and married her. So it happened that John's family seemed to grow smaller as one after another married and started a new home—that is, the group about John's hearthstone grew smaller; but each wedding brought another loved one into the circle of John and Betty's love. So their family really grew larger.

. . . . As each of the five eldest children was married they received the money left them by their Uncle Robert, and it was a great help to these young couples. With it they bought their farms—paying no more than a dollar an acre for their land—all within six miles of their father's farm, and each couple started a new home in a new clearing, where they lived much the same sort of life that John and Betty had lived in their first years in Moresville.

. . . . John Taylor and his wife, Eleanor Laraway, lived on a farm about five miles west of Moresville. When Robert fell in love with Susanna Fellows he decided to build a home for her with his own hands before they were married. He went into the forest about three miles from his father's tavern and found a fine spring of water. Here he bought his land, made a clearing, and built a cabin, sleeping out-of-doors, sheltered only by a ledge of rocks while he was doing this work. When they were married he had the little cabin home all ready for his bride. . . . . When Alexander was grown he bought, as part of his farm, the very woods where, when he was a small boy, he had met and driven off the mother bear, and

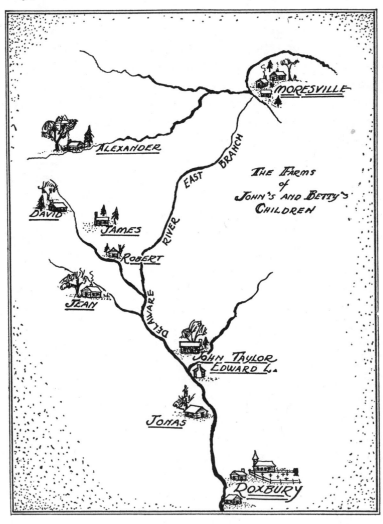

here he and his wife, Nancy Harley, made their home.
. . . . Jonas, always full of fun and good humor, and
a great favorite with everyone, took his bride, Deborah
Person, to a new claim near the present village of
Roxbury. Once, after they were grown men, he and
John Taylor both ran for the office of town supervisor.
There was great excitement over the race between the
brothers. Because Jonas was so well liked, he won the
election, but the two brothers were as good friends as
ever. The next day John Taylor invited Jonas to his
home to dinner, Jonas accepted the invitation, and they
had a good laugh over the close election.

. . . . Jean was a slim, bonny girl about fifteen when
David Smith, a young Scotchman who was a distant
relative of John's mother, and who had just come to
America from Forres, Scotland, came to Moresville and
stayed at John's tavern. I am sure you can guess what
happened. Jean and David fell in love, were married,
and lived happily ever after! They took up a new farm,
where they were next door neighbors of Robert and his
young bride.

. . . . If James were a young man nowadays, I suspect
he would be a college athlete, for he was very strong and ac-
tive, and was especially fond of wrestling. When he was
nineteen he was made lame by a contest in wrestling, and
was lame the rest of his life. He and his young wife, Rox-
anna Benjamin, lived on a farm near Jean's and Robert's.

. . . . When David was about twenty years old he did
as his older brothers had done—went into the wilderness, made a clearing, and built a home for his bride,
Elizabeth Gould. He bought his land from his father,
and it was near Jean's and Robert's and James's. So
many Mores lived here close together that the neighbor-

hood was called More Settlement. When David had been married some eight or ten years he decided to go west. With four other young men he started for Michigan, which was then the "Far West." They drove their teams to Buffalo, went to Detroit by boat, and then into Michigan on foot. They had exciting adventures which I can't tell you about now; and David nearly bought a farm, but he finally came back home from his long, adventuresome journey, satisfied to stay in his Catskill mountain home.

. . . . About the time that Edward L., the youngest of John's and Betty's children, was married, John built the first frame house in Moresville, a hotel, larger and better than the old one. Here Edward brought his bride, Charity Stanley, and Edward and his father ran the hotel together. It was not long until Betty had a stroke, which made her helpless the rest of her life. Charity was a sweet, faithful nurse through all the last fifteen years of Betty's life. In about five years after Betty's stroke Edward traded the hotel for John Taylor's farm, and Edward and his family, and his father and mother moved to the farm. It was here that John helped Edward build the Stone House, about which I will tell you in another story.

. . . . When John Taylor took his father's place as host in the hotel, he also took his father's position as postmaster and served for many years. When he was thirty-six years old, he was elected to the State Legislature and served there four terms as a member of the Assembly and one term as a Senator.

. . . . It was in 1786 that John and Betty brought 'heir family of six boys and a girl from Catskill to the place that became Moresville. It was in 1813, twenty-seven years later, that they left their well-loved home to spend their last years with Edward and Charity, near

Roxbury. In those twenty-seven years John and Betty had seen their sons grow into strong men, and their daughter into a beautiful woman, and had watched them go out from the home roof to homes of their own. They saw these new homes made happier with the laughter of little children, just as theirs had been. They saw their sons loved and respected by all their neighbors, and often holding public offices to which their neighbors selected them. . . . . They saw the County of Ulster divided and the part they lived in become Delaware County; they saw township lines changed so that Moresville was no longer in the town of Stamford, but was part of the town of Roxbury; they saw some of the trails become wagon roads, and a few of the fords crossed by bridges; and they saw many of the log cabins displaced by neat frame houses. What wonderful years those were—full of work and care, but full, too, of real adventure and accomplishment, for John and Betty and their children were doing their part in building a new country—America!

AROUND THE EVENING FIRE

IN the last story I told you about the evenings around the fireplace in John More's tavern, when John and some traveler-guest told stories while Betty knitted or mended. Let us forget, for a little time, that I have told you about the children growing up, while we go back and enjoy one of those cozy evenings with John and Betty, their children and their guests.

. . . . Outside John More's log-cabin tavern the ground was covered with a heavy snow and the bitter wind was whistling around the chimney, but inside the thick, log walls, with a huge fire of hickory logs burning brightly in the great stone fireplace, it was warm and friendly. The light from the fire and from several tallow candles played over the faces of the group about the fire, but left the corners of the big room in shadow. Several of the children sat on the rough, gray hearthstone close to the fire, roasting chestnuts and listening to the grown-ups talk.

. . . . Sometimes, when everything was still for a moment, they could hear in the forest not far away the fierce howl of a wolf or the shrill scream of a panther. But they were not frightened; they only drew closer to the fire, and glanced at their father with complete confidence in his ability to protect them from danger.

. . . . This evening the circle was made larger by three men who were stopping over night in John's cabin. Two were on their way from Catskill to a new settlement many miles deeper in the wilderness, and the third man was a trader or traveling peddler. He had come through snow and wind along a rough trail up the East Branch of the Delaware River from his last stopping place, near where Roxbury now stands. It was the end of a hard day's travel, and when these men had reached John's tavern they were nearly exhausted with the cold and the slow progress of their horses through the deep snow. But the warm fire and the good supper that Betty had served them revived their tired bodies and their worn spirits. Now the supper hour was over, and the children were greatly interested in the conversation around the blazing fire.

. . . . The howling of a wolf near the tavern turned the talk toward adventures with wild animals, that were so plentiful through all the woods, and the children, with ears and eyes open wide, forgot their chestnuts as they listened to the stories.

. . . . "Last summer, when I was over on the Charlotte River," began the trader, "I heard of a man named Gordon who had a strange sort of adventure with a bear—it was pretty serious, and yet it was sort of funny."

. . . . The trader paused to light his pipe, and the children almost stopped breathing—they were so afraid he wouldn't tell the story. But as soon as his pipe was going well, he went on.

. . . . "It happened in the spring, before the bears were well fed up after their winter's sleep. They were still pretty hungry and would go after a man if they had a chance. Gordon was alone, and was going along the trail through the woods when he came to the river, at a place where there was a log across the water, and he stepped out on the log to cross the river.

. . . . "He had taken only a few steps on the log when he saw a large bear start along the log from the other end. The bear had seen him, and was making good time toward him. Gordon is a big, husky fellow, and he had his axe, so he decided to fight the bear rather than try to run from him. They met, and Gordon struck the heaviest blow he could with his axe, but the bear warded it off with his great paw, knocked the axe out of young Gordon's hand, and it fell in the river.

. . . . "Then it was a matter of fighting the bear with his bare hands, and fight he did with all his might. The man and the bear fell into the river together, and Gordon found it mighty hard to escape from the angry animal. In the struggle the bear tore most of Gordon's clothes off him, and mashed his arm and hand terribly. When I saw him he was still crippled from the fight.

. . . . "Gordon doesn't remember just how he managed to escape from the big paws and the long arms of the angry beast and swim to shore. He dragged himself home, with his clothes torn to rags and his arm hanging helpless. He says he doesn't want to meet another hungry bear, especially in the middle of a river!"

. . . . The old peddler stopped, relit his pipe, and when the children looked at their roasted chestnuts, they found that the nuts were hopelessly burned.

. . . . This trader had stopped at John's tavern before, and John had learned that he was a good story-teller, with an almost endless supply of interesting tales. John and the other guests asked the old peddler to tell them another story of an adventure with wild animals; and stopping often to fill or to relight his pipe, he told them this tale he had heard on his travels through the country:

. . . . "Old man Webster, over on Rose's Brook, is one of the best hunters in the country, I reckon. I've heard it said that he'd rather shoot a buck than eat a good dinner. I'll tell you how he once shot a buck *for* his dinner—and on a Sunday, too.

. . . . "It seems that he and his neighbors all came into Delaware County from Connecticut and they keep the Sabbath very strictly, just as they did in Connecticut. It's very seldom that a preacher visits their settlement; so they manage their Sunday worship without a preacher, like the rest of the settlers—just as you do here, so I've heard. They meet at someone's house and sing and pray and read a sermon from a book of sermons that someone brought into the settlement from England or Scotland.

. . . . "Well, one pleasant Sabbath, last autumn, they were at Deacon Webster's for worship—old man Webster had been made a deacon—and the deacon was reading the sermon. He read the text, and had just started in on the sermon, when suddenly his black man, Amos, came to the open door, stopped, grinned broadly, and said to the deacon, 'Massa, massa, dar is a fine fat buck in the barnyard with the cattle.'

. . . . "Deacon Webster quietly laid down the book of sermons, picked up his rifle, stepped to the door, raised the gun to his shoulder, aimed, and—Bang! went the rifle, and down went the deer! The deacon told Amos to keep his eye on the deer for a few minutes to be sure it was dead; then old man Webster stepped back into the room, put up his rifle, picked up the book of sermons, and went on with his reading!

. . . . "That's the end of the deer, but not quite the end of the story. It was against their strict rules to go hunting on the Sabbath day. It happened that old Mr. Rose, who was Justice of the Peace, didn't go to the regular Sabbath worship that day; so he would not have known anything about the shooting if his wife hadn't happened to see it, for no one who saw the deacon do it would ever have made a complaint. Mrs. Rose was a long way from their house, but in sight of Deacon Webster's door, tending to a sick cow, when she heard the shot and saw the deer fall.

. . . . "She went back to her home and said to her husband, 'Esquire Rose, what do you think Deacon Webster has been doing?'

. . . . " 'I don't know, my dear,' said he, 'what has he?'

. . . . " 'Why, he has been shooting a deer on the Lord's day!' she told him, with great excitement and indignation.

. . . . "So the next morning Deacon Webster received a polite note from Justice Rose, charging him with his misdeed, and inviting him to call and pay the fine for shooting a deer on the Sabbath day. The deacon paid the fine, but he told some of his friends that he wouldn't have missed that good shot for twice the fine!"

. . . . The children joined in the laughter at the close of this story, and looked hopefully at the talkative trader, their eyes asking eagerly for another story. They had not long to wait—the short silence in the room was broken by a long howl from a hungry wolf in the forest and the trader chuckled softly.

. . . . "That wolf out yonder reminds me of another hunting story I heard up there on Rose's Brook—a story about a wolf. Want to hear it?"

. . . . There was a chorus of "Yes, yes," and when the old peddler had his pipe going to suit him, he began:

. . . . "There's a couple of brothers up there named Hotchkiss who are extra good hunters—don't seem to be afraid of anything, and are very clever at getting the best of an animal they are after, no matter what happens. Two or three winters ago the wolves were thick around there and were making lots of trouble killing sheep. These Hotchkiss fellows were on the watch for them all the time, and one morning discovered a fresh wolf track near their barn.

. . . . "They lost no time in getting their guns and starting on the trail of the animal. They followed this trail for several hours and had begun to wonder where on earth it was going to take them, when they came to a place where the wolf had crawled into a very large hollow tree. They thought at first that the wolf had beaten them, for this tree was one that had broken off near the ground and had fallen directly down a steep hill.

. . . . "They saw there was little chance of killing the wolf by shooting into the crooked tree, and they had no axe to cut the tree down. But they are fellows who won't give up when they are after a wolf; so one of them tried the only possible way—though it was a mighty dangerous way.

[79]

. . . . "He crawled right into that hollow tree, holding his gun pointed in front of him! He worked his way along till he came to the crook in the tree; then he could just manage to make room enough to let a tiny bit of light in—and in this faint light he saw the glaring eyes of the wolf before him! He quickly pulled his gun up to his shoulder, pointing it down the shorter part of the tree where the wolf was hiding, and fired!

. . . . "Then he backed out of the tree as fast as he could, not knowing whether he had killed the wolf, or whether the angry animal would be piling on his head any instant. He got out safely, then reloaded his gun, and again crawled through that hollow tree, feeling his way with his gun all the while.

. . . . "When he reached the crook in the tree he was especially careful, but there seemed to be no sound or movement coming from the animal; so he crawled a little farther, and touched the wolf with his rifle. The animal did not move—he poked the wolf harder, and still he showed no signs of life.

. . . . "Young Hotchkiss then knew that he had killed the wolf. He reached forward with his hand, got hold of the wolf's ears, and pulled. It took a lot of hard pulling to get that dead wolf out of the hollow tree, but Hotchkiss finally got him out and found him to be a huge animal.

. . . . "As for myself, I think I should rather have been the Hotchkiss brother who watched the affair than the one who went into the hollow tree after the wolf!"

. . . . As the old trader knocked the ashes from his pipe into the fireplace, Betty told the younger children that it was getting late for them, and they must go to bed. But they begged for one more story; and they begged so hard that their sweet mother yielded, and said they might stay up a little while longer if their guest would tell them another story. The trader was pleased that the children liked his tales, and asked them what sort of story they wanted to hear. There was a moment of silence before one of the boys answered.

. . . . "I'd like a story about a panther. That's the scariest animal I know."

. . . . "Let me see," said the old man slowly. "Do I know a story about a panther?" He thought a few moments, and then spoke again.

. . . . "Sure enough! I'd most forgotten this one, for it's a good many years since I heard it. This happened way over in the town of Andes. A panther had been making a great deal of trouble, killing cattle and sheep, and some of the younger men in the settlement decided they would get rid of the beast. Three of the men started out early one morning—Daniel Burr and Moses Earl and Samuel Jackson. They had no trouble following the panther's trail from the place where he had killed a sheep the night before to his den in the mountain a couple of miles away.

. . . . "They sent their dogs into the cave to rout the panther out, but the dogs went in about twelve feet and then refused to go any further. At this place the opening of the den became no more than a crack in the rock, and it made a rather sudden turn toward the left—and all that was beyond was in deep darkness.

. . . . "The panther did not like this disturbance just outside his den, and every few minutes he sent forth loud and angry snarls. Soon the dogs not only refused to go into the den, but backed entirely away from the opening.

[81]

. . . . "When the hunters found that they could not get the panther out where they could shoot him, young Jackson decided to go into the den after the panther. Burr and Earl tried to persuade him to give up this notion, but nothing could make him change his mind. He did permit his anxious friends to tie a rope around one of his legs so that they could pull him out quickly if it seemed necessary. Then he loaded his rifle, stuck a little candle down between the ends of a split stick, lighted the candle, and went into the panther's den.

. . . . "The entrance was so small that he had to creep along on his elbows and knees, and this was very difficult when he also had to drag his gun along with one hand and carry the lighted candle in the other. When he reached the turn in the little passage—the place where the dogs refused to go any further—he saw the angry panther only some twelve feet in front of him, sitting on its haunches, gnashing its teeth and snarling furiously!

. . . . "Jackson was surely in a very bad position for using a gun, but he managed to get his rifle in position so that he could shoot; then he aimed at the panther's head, and pulled the trigger. Young Burr and Earl, waiting at the entrance to the den, heard the roar of the gun and the howl of the wounded panther, and they decided that the time had come to use the rope on Jackson's leg!

. . . . "So they pulled, and they pulled, till they pulled him out of the cave and right to their feet. Poor Sam Jackson was a sorry sight! The sharp angles of the rocks had torn his clothes almost entirely off, and had taken a lot of skin as well! Jackson was as "mad as a hornet" because the other men had pulled him out! He wanted to stay and finish off the panther while he was there. In the den the panther was roaring with pain; in front of the den Jackson was swearing with anger! It was hard to tell which was the most furious!

. . . . "After a time, when the smoke had cleared away from the cave, Moses Earl followed Sam's trail into the cave. One well-aimed shot and the panther fell motionless. He waited a little while—the panther showed no signs of life—then he crawled into the den, fastened a rope about the panther's legs, and with the help of his friends on the outside, at the other end of the rope, pulled the dead animal out of the den. It proved to be a full-grown panther, and the whole settlement was grateful to the three young men who had killed it. For some time there were no more cattle and sheep killed by panthers in that locality, but it was a long, long time before Samuel Jackson's skin was whole again."

. . . . The old man was silent a moment; then he said, "Now you youngsters get into your beds, and I hope you won't dream of the wolves and panthers I've been telling you about."

. . . . The children said "Good-night," and went off to bed, trembling with the excitement of the stories they had heard, and I think it quite likely that they did dream of those wild animals! And if the boys and girls who are great-great-great-great-grandchildren of those pioneer children read these hunting stories just before they go to bed, I shouldn't be surprised if they too will dream of the bears and wolves and panthers that roamed through the woods near John More's cabin home!

ALONG THE SUNSET TRAIL

N another story I have told you that John and Betty left the hotel at Moresville after Betty became helpless, and that they went, with Edward and Charity, to live in the red house on the road between Moresville and Roxbury. Here, surrounded with the love and care of their children and grandchildren, they spent their last years, going down the sunset trail to the setting of the sun of life.

. . . . Betty was a patient invalid, lovingly cared for by Charity, and John was busy helping Edward to improve the farm. East of the house there was a little trout brook that had two waterfalls—the "big falls" and the "little falls" they were called. Below the big falls John built a trough that carried part of the water to an overhead wheel, and this ran the machinery of a saw-mill. The saw-mill John built also, and here he cut all the lumber that Edward needed and most of the lumber their neighbors used as well. Several of these neighbors were John's children, for Edward's house was near More Settlement. John spent many busy days running the saw-mill, cutting lumber for Robert or James or David or Jean's husband, David Smith, or perhaps for some neighbor who was not a More, but for whom he was happy to do a friendly service.

. . . . Just above the little falls John built a dam across the brook, and a small ditch that carried some of this stored-up water down near the house, where it ran a churn. This saved Charity many hours of tiresome labor churning the butter.

. . . . Edward wanted to raise apples and pears and other orchard fruit on his farm; so with his father's help he set out and grafted many fruit trees. After they were growing well, John pruned them, and carefully watched them till they were well-grown and were bearing delicious fruit.

. . . . In the homes of his children John saw his many grandchildren growing up without a school, and this made him unhappy. Since he no longer had the care of the hotel, and did not have the entire care of this farm he decided that he had time to teach these children himself. So he gathered the grandchildren together into a school, and invited the other neighbors to send their children—without cost to any of the parents. So John became a teacher, and did the best he could to give these children the beginnings of an education. After a few years a public school was built about a half-mile up the valley, and John's pupils went to that school.

. . . . Ten years John and Betty had lived here in Edward's home when the first break came in the family circle—when Betty, the sweet, gentle mother and grandmother passed away and left a sorrowing family. She was buried in the corner of the orchard that stood on a little knoll northeast of the house; and here John, lonely for his dearly-loved Betty, often came at twilight to be just a little nearer his dear one.

The Stone House . . . . A few years after Betty's death Edward decided to build a new house, larger than the red house, and of stone. He hired a number of men to get the stones out of the pasture and from the hillside, and to haul them where the house was to stand; and he hired stone-masons to do the cutting of the stones and the actual building. It was one of the finest houses in that part of the country: downstairs a parlor, guest bed-room, family sitting room, Edward's and Charity's room, a kitchen, and Grandfather's room; upstairs a very large bedroom for all the girls of the family, and another for the boys; and over the kitchen the attic and servant-girl's quarters. Grandfather's room was in the southeast corner, off a small porch, and also opened into the kitchen. . . . . John helped with the building of the house, especially with cutting the stones and making them ready to build into the walls. On one stone, larger than the rest, he carved "E. M. Built 1829.", and this stone was set in the wall, just over the front door, which faced the Delaware River. Sometime, when you go to see this house, you will see this stone with John's carving of Edward's initials on it. The stone house was strong and well-built, like the houses that John had lived in when a boy in Scotland, and it was a comfortable home for Edward's family. . . . . During the summer, while the men were building this house, the women were busy, too. Charity, with the help of her oldest daughter, Elizabeth, and one hired girl, did all the cooking and other housework for this huge family, including the workmen, and in addition they spun and wove a hundred yards of woolen cloth and a hundred yards of linen cloth, and made a new yarn carpet for the parlor of the new house. It seems almost impossible!

A Welcome Visitor . . . . The years passed quietly and slowly for John. He missed Betty keenly, and spent much of his time visiting his sons and his daughter, Jean, going to each home for a visit of a week or ten days. His grandchildren loved him dearly, and were eager for his visits. They were very happy when they looked up the road and saw Grandfather coming—a rather small man, with white hair, a friendly smile, very polite manners, and a quick, vigorous step.

. . . . "Grandfather is coming! Grandfather is coming!" the children shouted, as they ran to meet him.

. . . . "Good mornin', sonnie! Good mornin', lassie! Are ye weel?" Grandfather greeted them, and they all went into the house while Grandfather greeted the rest of the family.

. . . . Grandfather always wanted to know how each child was doing in school, and he often helped them with some hard lesson. They especially liked to have him help them with their writing. First they brought him a strong goose or turkey quill, and John made a fine quill pen of it. He had a small, very sharp knife that he carried in a little leather case, and never used for anything but to cut quill pens.

. . . . When the pen was ready, and the ink and paper were brought out, John wrote copies for the children; and very fine copies they were, for his writing was as plain and clear as any print. It was a proud child who could show Grandfather at his next visit his pages of writing of the copies neatly done; and a "Weel done, laddie!" or a "Weel done, lassie!" from Grandfather was as good a reward as a child could ask.

. . . . When evening came, the children liked to sit about the big fireplace while Grandfather told them of his boyhood in Scotland, of his voyage across the sea, and of his early days in America.

. . . . One day, when John was visiting at David's home, he was sharpening knives for Elizabeth, and John Osborn, David's oldest child, was turning the grindstone for him. Many times little John Osborn had heard his grandfather tell of his life in Scotland, and of his early years in America, but the boy had never had a chance to ask his grandfather the questions that were in his mind. This was his chance.

. . . . "Grandfather," he asked, "why did you leave all the comforts and pleasures of Scotland and come to this country with its forests full of Indians and wild animals?"

. . . . "Johnny, it was like this," Grandfather answered, as he lifted the knife off the grindstone, "In Scotland the people were divided into classes, and the lords owned all the land. I went to school and found I could learn as well as any, and I made up my mind, Johnny, that if there was a place on God's green earth where one mon was as good as another mon, I'd find it. So I decided to go to America, where I, too, could own land and be a lord."

. . . . "But why did you go so far back in the forest, Grandfather?" questioned the boy.

. . . . Grandfather stopped again, and looking up at the beautiful, tall trees he answered, "Johnny, I watched the tree growth, and went on and on till I reached a place where the trees were so big and strong that I knew the right kind of soil was there. And there we stopped."

. . . . John Osborn never forgot this talk with Grandfather, and when he was a grown man, he often told his own children about it.

. . . . Grandfather liked to go to Jonas' home, for many settlers came to Jonas' grist-mill and saw-mill on business, and John enjoyed visiting with these old friends and neighbors, many of whom used to come to the hotel in Moresville while John lived there. While the men waited for their grist to be ground, or for the lumber to be cut to complete their loads, stories of the early days were exchanged, stories both serious and gay.

. . . . One day when John's son Alexander was there, they were talking about the times before Jonas' grist-mill was built. The nearest grist-mill was then far away, over across the Bearkill, and Alexander told how he and his son used to go there to have their grist ground. On horseback, through the wilds of the Bearkill, they carried their wheat and corn to be ground. It was such a long trip that darkness fell long before they were back at home, and as they came through the deep woods, the wolves were howling about them—often so close that it was very terrifying. Then the other men in the group told similar tales of their earlier experiences.

. . . . One day John went to visit a grandchild, John P., a son of Jonas. There was a new baby in John P.'s home, and Grandfather wanted to see this little great-grandchild. When the baby's mother opened the door and greeted John, he said, "I cam to see if the mither and the wee bairnies are weel."

. . . . "Yes, Grandfather," the baby's mother answered, "just see what a fine baby we have." And she placed the tiny baby on the old man's knee.

. . . . "And what is his name?" asked Grandfather.

. . . . "We have named him Owen Wicks More—a fine big name for such a little boy, isn't it?" replied the mother.

[89]

. . . . But John was too much taken up with the baby to answer her question. After a few minutes he looked up and said, "Mither, he's na a strong laddie. I hae my dout ye raise him."

. . . . But this was one time, boys and girls, that John More made a mistake, for the mother did raise that baby, and Owen Wicks More lived to be a very old man, and was still telling this story when he was nearly ninety years old!

. . . . John always liked to walk: he walked when he went to visit a relative, and he walked to church in Roxbury, although, as he grew older, it was too far for him to walk on Sunday morning before church service. So he walked to Jonas' home on Saturday, then to church on Sunday morning, back to Jonas' after service, and on Monday back to Edward's. And he rarely missed a Sabbath service!

. . . . One day when John was walking to Roxbury to visit his grandson Richard, who was Edward's oldest son, he had a strange experience. When he arrived at Richard's he told the family about it: how a black dog had come out at him and seemed determined to bite him. He found he could not drive the dog off, and though he was sorry to do it, he finally had to kill the animal with his "stick" as he called his cane.

. . . . A little later a neighbor who had just come over the same road stopped in and told how he had seen a dead fox by the roadside. Richard asked him just where it was, and they found that the dead fox was lying just where Grandfather said he had killed the dog. Then they knew what had happened—Grandfather's eyes were not so good as they used to be, and he had killed the fox, thinking it was a dog. At just that time many foxes were being bitten by mad dogs, and doubtless the reason this fox attacked the old man was that it was a mad fox—just as dangerous as a mad dog!

. . . . Soon after Jonas's daughter Mary married Edward Burhans, Grandfather went to visit her, and was greatly surprised to see her without a cap, for in those days every married woman always wore a cap. John asked her how it happened that she was not wearing a cap, like other married women, and with considerable spirit, she told him.

. . . . "I don't want to wear caps, so before I was married, I didn't make any. Mother was determined that I should wear them, and a few days after Edward and I were married mother came to see us and was carrying a box. When Edward asked her what was in it, she said, very sternly, 'Caps for my daughter'."

. . . . "Edward answered her, 'My wife shall wear no cap on her pretty hair'."

. . . . "Mother, so determined I must wear caps, stood her ground. 'But all married women wear them, and I have made these especially fine'."

. . . . "Edward still insisted that he didn't want me to cover my hair with a cap. And I don't want to wear one—so I'm not going to!"

. . . . Grandfather laughed softly, but he never told Mary whether he approved of her new ideas.

. . . . When John was at Edward's home he spent many hours at a labor of love and devotion—carving Betty's tombstone. From the ledges of stone on the hillside back of the house, he took a big, flat, sandstone slab, then slowly and carefully carved on it the simple words telling of Betty's life and death, and lovingly helped lay the stone over Betty's grave. Then he took another slab just like this one and carved it for his own grave.

. . . . The children—many of them his grandchildren and great-grandchildren—as they passed on their way to school, liked to stop and watch the gentle, old man while he painstakingly cut the letters. When they had watched as long as they could without being late for school, they hurried on to the little schoolhouse a half-mile up the valley from the stone house, usually going through the stony pasture, and playing a game as they went.

. . . . The stony pasture was well-named, for there were so many stones in it, and the game was to see if they could go from the stone house to the school without stepping on the grass. By wisely choosing the way and making some rather long jumps from stone to stone, it could be done.

. . . . The school-house stood on a great rock, which sloped away from the front and side of the building. In winter this sloping rock was covered with ice, and then the children had wonderful times, sliding down it on boards, or home-made sleds, or even on tin pans! Many years later, the great naturalist, John Burroughs, went to school there, and played the same games and had the same sort of good times that John's grandchildren had.

. . . . The years went by. The sunset trail was growing shorter for John, and he knew that any year might be his last upon earth. Each year he wrote to some of his relatives in Scotland telling them of his health, and he wrote and gave to John Taylor the sort of notice of his death that he wanted sent, when he died, to his brother David in Scotland. John was getting ready for the end of his earthly journey.

. . . . He talked with his children about where he wished to be laid to rest. They felt that it should be in the Roxbury Cemetery, and when they said this to him, he thought of the promise Betty made him so many years ago in Scotland: "Whither thou goest, I will go; and wither thou lodgest, I will lodge: thy people shall be my people, and thy God my God; where thou diest I will die, and there will I be buried." Then he answered his children, "Bury me where you will, but let Betty lie beside me."

. . . . The year 1839 was passing, and John was about to finish his own tombstone. Only the date of death was lacking. He carved the numbers 1 and 8 and then paused, not knowing whether to carve a 3 and complete 1839, or to carve a 4 and make it 1840. He was ninety-five years old, and doubted whether he would stay through the year 1839. He left the number unfinished. The year closed, and Grandfather was still living.

. . . . On New Year's Day of 1840 he seemed as well as ever. He ate the holiday dinner, but soon after, with a low cry, he fell into Edward's arms, and his long, useful life was ended. Thus came the end of the sunset trail for John More.

. . . . It was a very large family group that sadly followed his body to its last resting-place in the Roxbury Cemetery—all his children, and more than two hundred grandchildren and great-grandchildren. The next summer Betty's remains were moved from the little hillside burying ground to Roxbury.

. . . . There they rest, side by side in death as in life, with the stones John carved covering them, and both in the shadow of the big More monument, the granite for which was brought from Scotland, near Forres, where

John had lived as a boy and young man and where he had married Betty.

. . . . The John and Betty stories are ended, but I want to give you part of a letter that John wrote just a few years before he died. He wrote this to a grandson who was working in New York City, but I believe he would like to say the same thing to each of us great-great-great-grandchildren, and great-great-great-great-grandchildren, and grandchildren with any number of greats!

. . . . Listen then, while John More speaks to you:

. . . . "I wish and advise that you be scrupulously honest and obliging to your employers, and complaisant and attentive to customers. I advise you to attend public worship on the Sabbath, and to pray morning and evening for grace to enlighten you, enable and assist you to love and fear God.

Your affectionate Grandfather,
John More."

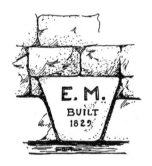

Books That Helped the Author Write These Stories

HISTORY OF THE MORE FAMILY, David Fellows More. *Published in Binghamton, New York*, by Samuel P. More. 1893.

THE HISTORICAL JOURNALS OF THE MORE FAMILY. April, 1892, to November, 1927. Issued by the John More Association.

HISTORY OF DELAWARE COUNTY, Jay Gould. *Published in Roxbury, New York*, by Kenny and Gould. 1856.

A REVOLUTIONARY PILGRIMAGE, Ernest Peixotto. *Published in New York City* by C. Scribner's Sons. 1917.

THE PICTURESQUE HUDSON, Clifton Johnson. *Published in New York City* by The Macmillan Company. 1909.

THE HUDSON RIVER, Edgar Mayhew Bacon. *Published in New York City* by G. P. Putnam's Sons. 1902.

RAMBLES IN COLONIAL BYWAYS—VOL. I., Rufus Rockwell Wilson. *Published in Philadelphia* by J. B. Lippincott Company. 1901.

SOCIAL NEW YORK UNDER THE GEORGES, Esther Singleton. *Published in New York City* by D. Appleton and Company. 1902.

NEW YORK—NOT SO LITTLE AND NOT SO OLD, Sarah M. Lockwood. *Published in Garden City* by Doubleday, Page and Company. 1926.

AMERICAN INDIANS, Frederick Starr. *Published in Boston* by D C. Heath and Company. 1898.

LEGENDS OF THE IROQUOIS TOLD BY THE CORNPLANTER, W. W. Canfield. *Published in New York City* by A. Wessels and Company. 1902.

WIGWAM STORIES, Mary Catherine Judd. *Published in Boston* by Ginn and Company. 1901.

BOYS AND GIRLS OF COLONIAL DAYS, Carolyn Sherwin Bailey. *Published in Chicago* by A. Flanagan Company. 1923.

IN THE CATSKILLS, John Burroughs. *Published in Boston* by Houghton Mifflin Company. 1910.

MY BOYHOOD, John Burroughs. *Published in Garden City, New York*, by Doubleday, Page and Company. 1922.

ROGERS-KELLOGG-STILLSON COMPANY
NEW YORK